FLORI

MW00647441

Fifth Edition

Carol M. Bast, Esq.

Upper Saddle River, New Jersey

Columbus, Ohio

Editor in Chief: Vernon Anthony
Acquisitions Editor: Gary Bauer
Editorial Assistant: Megan Heintz
Senior Managing Editor: JoEllen Gohr
Project Manager: Christina Taylor
Senior Operations Supervisor: Pat Tonneman
Art Director: Diane Ernsberger
Director of Marketing: David Gesell
Marketing Manager: Leigh Ann Sims
Marketing Assistant: Les Roberts
Copyeditor: Marianne L'Abbate

THE INFORMATION PROVIDED IN THIS TEXT IS NOT INTENDED AS LEGAL
ADVICE FOR SPECIFIC SITUATIONS, BUT IS MEANT SOLELY FOR
EDUCATIONAL AND INFORMATIONAL PURPOSES. READERS SHOULD
RETAIN AND SEEK THE ADVICE OF THEIR OWN LEGAL COUNSEL IN
HANDLING SPECIFIC LEGAL MATTERS.

13   17
ISBN-13: 978-0-13-502588-8
ISBN-10:   0-13-502588-5

CONTENTS

This book is designed for students of the law and those contemplating a legal career. It provides basic state-specific information on Florida state courts, persons involved with the state court system, alternative dispute resolution, and legal research. The book can be used effectively in an introductory law class as well as in civil procedure, criminal justice, and legal research classes.

The text is user-friendly and readable while providing necessary detail. Certain information is presented in charts and diagrams distributed throughout the book. Rule 9.800 of the Florida Rules of Appellate Procedure, containing the legal citation rules for court documents, is found in Appendix A.

Appendix B includes a list of URLs useful in conducting legal research or in learning more about the three branches of government. For example, the Office of the State Courts Administrator's home page, http://www.flcourts.org, contains a wealth of information concerning Florida courts. The Florida legislature's website, http://www.leg.state.fl.us, contains information on legislation and members of the Florida legislature. Appendix E contains questions regarding a number of the websites listed in Appendix B. Appendix C contains questions on cases decided by Florida state courts, and Appendix D contains questions concerning Florida Statutes. The questions may be answered by using sources available in your law library or by using online databases.

Florida Courts is designed as a textbook for classroom use. The information contained herein is intended only for educational and informational purposes.

Carol M. Bast

Florida Constitution

Florida has experienced six different constitutions during its history. Florida became a state in 1845, and the Constitution of 1838 became its first state constitution. The Constitution of 1838 was followed by the Constitutions of 1861, 1865, 1868, and 1885. The Constitution of 1986, as amended, is Florida's current constitution.[1]

Article III of the **Florida Constitution** vests legislative power in the **Florida Legislature**, composed of the **Senate** and **House of Representatives**.[2] The sixty-day regular legislative session generally begins on the first Tuesday after the first Monday in March. A special session of the Florida Legislature may be called by the governor or as provided by law.[3] Article IV vests the executive power in the **governor**.[4] The governor must be at least thirty years old and must have resided in Florida the preceding seven years. The governor is limited to two consecutive terms.[5]

Article V of the Constitution of 1885 was carried forward as Article V of the Constitution of 1986 until a revised Article V became effective on January 1, 1973.[6] Prior to 1973, the Florida court system was much more complex than it is today, with Florida having a greater variety of trial courts than any state except New York.[7] Article V of the current constitution vests judicial power in the **supreme court**, the **district courts of appeal**, the **circuit courts**, and the **county courts**.[8]

The Florida constitution calls for a **Constitutional Revision Commission** to comprehensively review the constitution ten years after it was first enacted and each twenty years thereafter. The Constitutional Revision Commission examines the constitution and proposes amendments to the constitution to be voted upon by Florida voters.[9] In 2017 the next Constitutional Revision Commission will be conducting a comprehensive review of the Florida constitution.[10]

Interplay among the three branches

The Florida **legislative, executive,** and **judicial branches** divide the powers of the Florida state government and check and balance each other.[11] The Florida legislature passes **statutes** that are interpreted by the courts and are executed by the executive branch.

The courts declare a statute unconstitutional if it is contrary to the
Florida constitution or the United States Constitution. The courts also
produce **common law** (also referred to as **case law**). Common law
governs in areas, such as defamation, that are not covered by statute.
The governor appoints judges to vacancies on the Florida District
Courts of Appeal and appoints justices to vacancies on the Florida
Supreme Court. **Administrative agencies**, such as the Department
of Health and the Department of Law Enforcement, are part of the
executive branch.[12] They promulgate **rules and regulations** that
have the force of law.

State Courts

Relationship to federal courts

Both Florida state courts and United States district courts are present
within the state. The Florida courts handle matters concerning the
Florida constitution, Florida statutes, common law, and court rules.
The federal courts handle matters concerning federal statutes and the
United States Constitution. In addition, federal courts have **diversity
jurisdiction**.[13] Diversity jurisdiction allows a person from one state
to sue a person from another state in federal district court if the matter
in controversy is more than $75,000. Thus, a lawsuit involving a
large sum of money and parties from different states could be filed
either in state or federal court. A case originally filed in state court
may be **removed** to federal court if the federal court has diversity
jurisdiction or the case involves a federal statute or the United States
Constitution. In a diversity case, the federal court must apply
applicable state law, and a United States Court of Appeals or the
United States Supreme Court may consult the Florida Supreme Court
on a question of Florida law. The federal court does this by
certifying a question of law to the Florida Supreme Court.[14]

The trial level federal court is the **United States district court**.
Three United States district courts serve Florida. A map of the three
federal districts in Florida is accessible through the federal courts
website at http://www.uscourts.gov/.

∞   The **United States District Court for the Northern
     District of Florida** holds court in Gainesville, Marianna,
     Tallahassee, Panama City, and Pensacola.

∞ The **United States District Court for the Middle District of Florida** holds court in Fernandina, Ft. Myers, Jacksonville, Live Oak, Ocala, Orlando, St. Petersburg, and Tampa.
∞ The **United States District Court for the Southern District of Florida** holds court in Ft. Lauderdale, Ft. Pierce, Key West, Miami, and West Palm Beach.[15]

Appeals from the United States district courts in Florida, Georgia, and Alabama go to the **United States Court of Appeals for the Eleventh Circuit**, which holds court in Atlanta, Jacksonville, and Montgomery.[16] Generally, a case that began in Florida would reach the **United States Supreme Court** either from the United States Court of Appeals for the Eleventh Circuit or from the Florida Supreme Court by a **petition for writ of certiorari** being accepted by the United States Supreme Court.[17] Cases heard by the United States Supreme Court generally involve questions of federal law or questions concerning the United States Constitution. The jurisdiction of the United States Supreme Court is largely discretionary. Only a very small percentage of the cases for which writs of certiorari are sought are ever heard by the United States Supreme Court.

The Florida State–Federal Judicial Council recognized that an attorney might be scheduled to appear in state and federal court at the same time, thus creating a calendar conflict. To deal with calendar conflicts, the council adopted the following priorities:[18]

∞ Criminal cases should prevail over civil cases.
∞ Jury trials should prevail over nonjury trials.
∞ Appellate arguments, hearings, and conferences should prevail over trials.
∞ The case in which the trial date has been first set should take precedence.
∞ Circumstances such as cost, numbers of witnesses and attorneys involved, travel, length of trial, age of case, and other relevant matters may warrant deviation from this policy. Such matters are encouraged to be resolved through communication between the courts involved.

Televising court proceedings

The presiding judge may limit television cameras and photographic cameras to

∞   control the conduct of proceedings before the court.
∞   ensure decorum and prevent distractions.
∞   ensure the fair administration of justice in the pending cause.[19]

State attorney

Each judicial circuit has a **state attorney** elected for a four-year term. The state attorney must have been a member of the bar for the preceding five years and must live within the circuit. The state attorney position is full-time, and a state attorney may not practice law.[20] The state attorney is the attorney representing the State of Florida at the trial level. The state attorney participates in civil and criminal cases in the circuit and county courts, prosecuting or defending on behalf of the state.[21] The state attorney attends the grand jury to

∞   examine witnesses before the grand jury.
∞   give legal advice to the grand jury.
∞   prepare indictments.[22]

In addition, the state attorney assists the Florida Attorney General with civil and criminal appeals in which the state is a party from the respective circuit to the Florida Supreme Court.[23] The state attorney is assisted by **assistant state attorneys** appointed by the state attorney.[24] **Municipal prosecutors** may prosecute municipal ordinances if they are so authorized.[25]

Public defender and capital collateral representative

Each judicial circuit has a **public defender** elected for a four-year term. The public defender must have been a member of the Florida Bar for the preceding five years and must live within the circuit.[26] The public defender represents a defendant who is indigent and who is

∞   charged with or is under arrest for a felony;
∞   charged with a misdemeanor, a traffic violation, or a violation of a municipal or county ordinance punishable with imprisonment;
∞   alleged to be a delinquent child;
∞   petitioned to be institutionalized as mentally ill; or
∞   petitioned to be involuntarily admitted as having developmental disabilities.

The public defenders of the second, seventh, tenth, eleventh, and fifteenth judicial circuits handle felony appeals to state and federal courts. The public defender is assisted by **assistant public defenders**.[27]

At times more than one defendant in a case needs public defender assistance. If the interests of the defendants are so adverse that the public defender cannot represent multiple defendants, the court may appoint private attorneys to represent one or more of the defendants.[28]

The **capital collateral representative** represents any indigent in the state who has been sentenced to death and whose direct appeals have terminated. The capital collateral representative is involved in any "collateral actions challenging the legality of the judgment and sentence."[29]

Court rules

The law is composed of **substantive law** and **procedural law**. Substantive law defines rights and duties (legal claims and obligations). Procedural law governs the process of courts dealing with those rights and duties. For example, the Florida statute allowing the government to punish someone for murder is a substantive law. The speedy trial rule, which generally compels the defendant to be brought to trial within 175 days of arrest, is a procedural law.

Although substantive law is important in court, judges and litigation attorneys must refer to **court rules** to determine how a case is to be handled. Court rules for use in Florida state courts are adopted by the Florida Supreme Court and may be repealed by two-thirds vote of the Florida Senate and two-thirds vote of the Florida House of Representatives.[30]

Basic rules at the trial level are the **Florida Rules of Civil Procedure**, the **Florida Rules of Criminal Procedure**, and the **Florida Evidence Code**. The Florida Rules of Civil Procedure apply to civil cases in Circuit Court and County Court, except those cases handled in Small Claims Court or in the probate or family law divisions of Circuit Court.[31] The Florida Rules of Civil Procedure govern the progress of the entire case, from service of process, to form of pleadings, to discovery, to trial, to judgment, to post-trial matters. A number of useful litigation forms are found at the end of the rules.

The **Florida Probate Rules** govern probate and guardianship proceedings. The Florida Rules of Civil Procedure are applicable in probate and guardianship proceedings only as provided in the Florida Probate Rules.[32] The **Florida Small Claims Rules** govern civil cases in County Court where the amount in controversy does not exceed $5,000, exclusive of costs, interest, and attorney's fees. Specified Florida Rules of Civil Procedure also govern in Small Claims Court.[33]

The **Florida Rules of Criminal Procedure** govern procedure in criminal cases, and in traffic court, as made applicable by the **Rules of Traffic Court.**[34] The Florida Rules of Criminal Procedure govern the progress of the criminal case, from preliminary proceedings, to arraignment and pleas, to discovery, to trial, to verdict, to post-trial matters, to sentence. Forms for use in criminal cases are found at the end of the rules.

The **Family Law Rules of Procedure** became effective January 1, 1996.[35] The rules apply to "all actions concerning family matters, including actions concerning domestic, repeat, dating, and sexual violence, except as otherwise provided by the Florida Rules of Juvenile Procedure or the Florida Probate Rules."[36] The Florida Rules of Civil Procedure apply in family law matters except as otherwise provided in the Family Law Rules.[37] The Florida Evidence Code applies to family law matters and governs if there is a conflict between the Code and the Family Law Rules.[38] Section II of the Family Law Rules contains "forms, commentary, and instructions." This section assists one not represented by an attorney.[39]

The **Florida Evidence Code** governs the **admissibility of evidence** at trial. Evidence admitted should be relevant, reliable, and not unduly prejudicial or likely to cause confusion.[40] Some conversations, such as those between attorney and client, are privileged. **Privileged conversations** are inadmissible unless a person holding the privilege **waives** (relinquishes) the privilege by voluntarily disclosing the conversation or consenting to disclosure.[41] In contrast to the other court rules described in this section, the Florida Evidence Code, because it is both substantive and procedural in nature, is enacted by the Florida Legislature and then adopted by the Florida Supreme Court.[42]

The **Florida Rules of Appellate Procedure** govern appellate proceedings in circuit court (when functioning as an appellate court), in the district courts of appeal, and in the Florida Supreme Court.[43] The rules deal with matters such as the jurisdiction of the appellate courts, form of briefs filed with the court, oral argument, and *amicus curiae*.[44] *Amicus curiae* means "friend of the court." An organization or person not a party to a case may wish to file a brief to present the court with additional information. The court may allow the organization or person to file a brief as *amicus curiae*.

Court rules undergo a comprehensive review every three years, with one-third of the committees reporting each year. By December 15 of the year prior to the reporting year, the Board of Governors of the Florida Bar will have voted whether to reject, accept, or amend rule changes proposed by the committees and submitted by October 15 of the year prior to the reporting year. By February 1 of the reporting year, the committees will report their proposed changes to the Florida Supreme Court. The Florida Supreme Court will hear oral argument on the proposed amendments in May or June of the reporting year, and amendments will be approved to take effect on January 1 of the year following the reporting year.[45]

In addition to other applicable court rules, most courts have **local rules** and **administrative orders**. The local rules supplement other court rules. Administrative orders usually deal with matters such as assignment of judges to divisions. The local rules and administrative orders apply only within the jurisdiction of the particular court. Local rules of trial courts are proposed by at least a majority of the judges in the circuit, are submitted to the local bar, and are submitted to the Florida Supreme Court for approval. Once approved by the Florida Supreme Court, the local rules become effective. A copy of the local rules is a **public record** and is available for inspection.[46]

Juries

There are two types of juries—grand juries and petit juries. The Florida Constitution guarantees:

> No person shall be tried for **capital crime**
> [punishable by death] without presentment or
> indictment by a grand jury, or for other felony
> without such presentment or indictment or an
> information under oath filed by the prosecuting
> officer of the court . . . .[47]

A **presentment** is a formal accusation of a crime made by the grand jury on its own motion. An **indictment** is a formal accusation of a crime made by a grand jury based on evidence presented to it. An **information** is a formal accusation of a crime made by the state attorney.

The **grand jury** is made up of fifteen to twenty-one persons. It investigates crimes, hears testimony, and receives evidence in secret before determining whether to issue an indictment. Twelve grand jurors need to concur to issue an indictment.[48]

In contrast to the grand jury, which determines whether someone should be charged, the **petit jury** tries the case. The Florida constitution guarantees trial by jury. "The right of trial by jury shall be secure to all and remain inviolate."[49] The number of jurors on a petit jury varies depending on the type of case. Civil cases require a six-person jury, except that **eminent domain** cases require a twelve-person jury.[50] (In eminent domain cases, the jury must determine how much a landowner should be paid for private land the government takes for a public purpose.) A criminal case punishable by death requires a twelve-person jury, while any other criminal case requires a six-person jury.[51] The verdict in a criminal case must be unanimous.[52]

Jurors can be of either sex, must be at least eighteen years old, must be legal residents of Florida, and have an address in the county in which they are called for jury duty. Jurors' names used to be selected from the list of registered voters. Jurors' names are now taken from Florida driver's license information. Anyone who does not have a driver's license but who desires to be eligible to serve as a juror can do so by filling out an **affidavit** (a written statement swearing to or affirming the information in the affidavit).[53] The following persons are disqualified from serving as jurors:

∞ someone who has been convicted of a felony, unless the person's civil rights have been restored, or one who is under prosecution for any crime.

∞ the governor, lieutenant governor, cabinet officers, clerks of court, and judges.

∞ a person who has an interest in the case.

Unless they choose to serve, law enforcement officers and investigators are excused from jury service. The following persons may be excused from jury service upon request:

∞ expectant mothers and parents not employed full-time with custody of a child younger than six.

∞ persons to whom jury service would be a hardship or extreme inconvenience or persons claiming public necessity.

∞ persons seventy or older.

∞ persons responsible for the care of an incapacitated person.

The judge has the discretion to excuse a practicing attorney, a practicing physician, and an infirm person.[54]

A list of potential jurors is selected at random by the clerk of the court. A **jury venire** (a group of prospective jurors) is selected at random from the jury list, and persons on the jury venire are summoned to court to attend as jurors by being mailed a written notice. The parties in a case select the jury to decide the case from the jury venire. The parties conduct a **voir dire examination** (questioning of prospective jurors to determine if they are qualified and acceptable). A prospective juror would be disqualified if the prospective juror is related to any party or attorney, has an interest in the case, has formed any opinion about the case, or is an employee or has been an employee of any party (**challenge for cause**). The parties may disqualify a set number of prospective jurors for any reason or for no reason at all (**peremptory challenges**).[55]

Judges

Each judge and justice is required to complete thirty hours of continuing judicial education every three years, two hours of which are dedicated to judicial ethics. In addition, each new trial judge must complete the Florida Judicial College program within the judge's first year of service. Each new district judge and justice must complete an

appellate judge education program within the first two years of
service.[56]

Florida judges and justices must comply with the **Code of Judicial
Conduct**. A breach of any of the ethical principles comprising the
code may subject a judge or justice to discipline imposed by the
Florida Supreme Court. The titles of the seven canons comprising the
code summarize the ethical obligations of judges and justices:

1. A Judge Should Uphold the Integrity and Independence of the
   Judiciary.
2. A Judge Should Avoid Impropriety and the Appearance of
   Impropriety in All of the Judge's Activities.
3. A Judge Shall Perform the Duties of Judicial Office Impartially
   and Diligently.
4. A Judge May Engage in Activities to Improve the Law, the Legal
   System, and the Administration of Justice.
5. A Judge Shall Regulate Extrajudicial Activities to Minimize the
   Risk of Conflict With Judicial Duties.
6. Fiscal Matters of a Judge Shall Be Conducted in a Manner that
   Does Not Give the Appearance of Influence or Impropriety . . . .
7. A Judge or Candidate for Judicial Office Shall Refrain From
   Inappropriate Political Activity.

In 2001, the Florida Supreme Court removed County Judge
McMillan from the bench for his alleged "improper conduct
including explicit statements indicating his bias for the State and
police in criminal prosecutions, and also misleading and false
statements regarding the local justice system, his opponent and others,
in violation of canons of the Code of Judicial Conduct."[57] In 2002,
the Florida Supreme Court admonished Judge Baker for requesting
computer information from consultants regarding a pending case
without involving the attorneys in the case, all in violation of the
discliplinary rules.[58]

Attorneys

The Florida Supreme Court regulates the admission of attorneys into
membership in the **Florida Bar** and the practice of law within
Florida.[59] Attorneys are deemed **officers of the court for the
administration of justice**.[60] This means that attorneys are treated

as if they were employees of the court and, as such, must conduct themselves in a manner that furthers justice. In contrast, other professions in Florida are regulated by the Florida Department of Business and Professional Regulation.[61]

Attorneys are prohibited from practicing law in Florida unless they are members of the **Florida Bar**. The Florida Bar is an involuntary bar association whose purpose is to "inculcate in its members the principles of duty and service to the public, to improve the administration of justice, and to advance the science of jurisprudence."[62] Attorneys admitted to practice in other states may be given permission to represent a client in a particular case in a Florida court.[63]

Attorneys practicing in Florida must be members of the Florida Bar and are subject to the **Rules Regulating the Florida Bar**. Chapter 3 of the rules is entitled **Rules of Discipline,** and Chapter 4 is entitled **Rules of Professional Conduct**. The Rules of Professional Conduct govern matters such as the attorney's duty to the client and to the court and the attorney's duty to avoid conflict of interest, as well as attorney advertising and solicitation and maximum fees in **contingency** cases. (In a contingency case, an attorney is paid a percentage of any amount recovered.) The preamble to the Rules of Professional Conduct states:

> A lawyer is a representative of clients, an officer of the legal system, and a public citizen having special responsibility for the quality of justice. . . . In all professional functions a lawyer should be competent, prompt, and diligent. . . . A lawyer's conduct should conform to the requirements of the law, both in professional service to clients and in the lawyer's business and personal affairs. . . . As a public citizen, a lawyer should seek improvement of the law, access to the legal system, the administration of justice, and the quality of service rendered by the legal profession.

A violation of the Rules of Professional Conduct is a cause for discipline. Discipline may range from admonishment, to probation, to public reprimand, to suspension, to **disbarment** (termination of the attorney's status as a member of the bar).[64] Typically, the bar receives

8,000 to 9,000 complaints against attorneys annually.[65] In the 2005–2006 fiscal year, the 8,736 disciplinary files opened resulted in fifty-two attorneys disbarred, twenty-nine publicly reprimanded, and sixteen admonished.[66]

Chapter 5 of the Rules Regulating the Florida Bar contains **Rules Regulating Trust Accounts**. The trust account rules govern the handling of money or property entrusted to the attorney. The rules also mandate that money that is small in amount or is to be held for a short time period and that is to be held in trust for a client is to be deposited into an interest-bearing trust account for the benefit of The Florida Bar Foundation, Inc.[67] The foundation provides public interest grants for legal aid to the poor, law student loans and scholarships, and improvements in the administration of justice.[68]

In 2004, the Florida Supreme Court revoked the conditional license of an attorney after the attorney failed to make child support payments.[69] In 2002, an attorney was sentenced to ten years in prison and twenty years probation after he took most of the $2.4 million proceeds of a loan he had helped his client obtain. The attorney resigned from the Florida Bar in 1998.[70]

Chapter 6 of the rules requires Florida Bar members to complete at least thirty hours of continuing education every three years. Chapter 6 also allows a Florida attorney to indicate an area of expertise as a "board certified" attorney.

Generally, an attorney may become "board certified" in certain areas of law by having practiced at least five years, passing an examination, and complying with other requirements.[71]

Although it is not mandated, many attorneys also join a local or special-interest bar association.

Pro se litigants

Some individuals choose to represent themselves in court. Generally, parties are allowed to appear ***pro se*** (unrepresented by an attorney). A party is required to be represented by an attorney in the following situations:

∞   Corporations and limited liability companies must be represented by an attorney, except that a corporate landlord's managing agent may file a case to evict a tenant for not paying rent.
∞   Unless the guardian of a minor or incompetent is an attorney, the guardian must be represented by an attorney.
∞   "A personal representative [person who administers a dead person's estate] of a decedent's estate must be represented by an attorney, unless the personal representative is an attorney or unless the personal representative is the sole person to receive assets from the estate."[72]

Legal assistants, paralegals, legal technicians

Legal assistant and **paralegal** are titles that refer to a person who works under the supervision of an attorney. The attorney remains ultimately responsible for the paralegal's or legal assistant's work. The terms are generally interchangeable. A **legal technician** generally refers to someone unsupervised by an attorney. A legal technician who goes beyond helping someone fill out Florida Supreme Court–approved forms and gives legal advice may be prosecuted for unlicensed practice of law. (See page 15 for further discussion on the unauthorized practice of law.)

Although a number of states have proposed licensing paralegals, legal assistants, or legal technicians to provide certain legal services without the supervision of an attorney, no state currently has such licensure.

Paralegals receive training in a variety of ways:

∞   on the job,
∞   by obtaining an associate of science degree in legal assisting from a Florida community college,
∞   by obtaining a bachelor's degree in legal studies, or
∞   by obtaining a certificate from a certificate-granting educational institution.

Legal assistants may call themselves **certified legal assistants** or **certified paralegals** by passing an examination offered by the **National Association of Legal Assistants** (NALA) and can become **certified Florida legal assistants** by first passing the NALA exam and then passing a Florida-specific exam offered by

Paralegal Association of Florida, Inc. (PAF) (formerly know as Florida Legal Assistants, Inc.), the Florida affiliate of NALA. The NALA exam is a fifteen-hour, two-day examination on federal law, and the PAF exam is a three-hour examination on Florida law. To maintain certification, the NALA-certified legal assistant must complete fifty hours of continuing education every five years, and the PAF-certified legal assistant must complete thirty hours of continuing legal education every five years.[73] Although these certifications are voluntary, a legal assistant may want to pursue certification by NALA or both NALA and PAF to indicate a comprehensive knowledge of the law, to obtain a legal assistant position, or to advance in employment.

As this book goes to press, it is anticipated that the Florida Supreme Court will adopt the Florida Registered Paralegal Program. The proposed program creates two categories of paralegals (the paralegal and the Florida Registered Paralegal), a paralegal code of ethics, and a disciplinary system. The Florida Registered Paralegal category is similar to a certified legal assistant because the Florida Registered Paralegal title requires a certain level of experience, education, and continuing education; however, compliance with the Florida Registered Paralegal criteria would be under the Florida Supreme Court rather than under paralegal organizations, as it is now for certified legal assistants.[74]

Florida Supreme Court–approved legal forms

Attorneys have long been criticized for pricing themselves out of the range of many individuals. With hourly rates at $100, $150, $200, and more per hour, many who need the services of an attorney cannot afford one. Until the 1990s, the Florida Supreme Court had approved only one legal form for use by nonattorneys. This was the **Contract for Purchase and Sale** used for real property transactions. That contract is a one-page form printed on legal-size paper. The main **negotiated** provisions, those bargained for between the parties, are specified in blanks on the front side of the contract, with the **Standard Terms and Conditions** printed on the reverse side. **Addenda** (pages containing other provisions) can be attached to the contract. The contract was so popular and so widely used, especially by real estate agents, that it became the standard contract for the sale of single-family residential properties.

In the early 1990s, the Florida Supreme Court finally approved other forms for use by nonattorneys. These forms include

∞ residential leases,
∞ dissolution of marriage forms,
∞ injunction for protection against violence forms,
∞ service and notice forms,
∞ child support forms,
∞ stepparent adoption forms, and
∞ landlord and tenant forms.

Nonattorneys may assist an individual in completing a Florida Supreme Court form without being engaged in unlicensed practice of law. The simplified forms attempt to provide the public access to the legal system while protecting the public from incompetency and fraud. The nonattorney is required to provide the individual with a disclosure form, signed by both the nonattorney and the individual, disclosing that the nonattorney is not an attorney and is not authorized to give legal advice or to represent the individual in court.[75]

Unauthorized practice of law

In Florida it is a third-degree felony for a nonattorney to practice law or make someone believe one is qualified to act as an attorney.[76] With the high cost of hiring an attorney, some laypersons may be tempted to turn to a "legal technician" or individual who offers to perform legal work much more cheaply than an attorney. A majority of the unauthorized practice of law cases involved immigration law.[77]

An attorney has graduated from three years of law school and has passed a bar examination. A person who hires an attorney who does not competently perform the requested legal services can file a grievance (a complaint) with the Florida Bar, which may result in the attorney being disciplined. It is also possible to sue the attorney for **malpractice** (failure of an attorney to act with the reasonable care ordinarily taken by attorneys). A portion of the Florida Bar annual dues is set aside in the **clients' security fund**. Money in the fund is used to reimburse clients for losses suffered from an attorney's "misappropriation, embezzlement, or other wrongful taking or conversion . . . of money or other property" that comes into "possession or control of" the attorney.[78]

A nonattorney may have had no formal training. If a nonattorney performs a legal service incompetently (as compared to an attorney), the nonattorney can be held liable only if the nonattorney's performance was unreasonable for a layperson.

The *local* unlicensed practice of law committee, the **circuit committee**, investigates any alleged unlicensed practice of law activities. The *statewide* unlicensed practice of law committee, the **standing committee**, evaluates the reports of the circuit committees and refers the matter to the **Florida Bar Board of Governors** (the governing body of the Florida Bar) to determine if the Florida Bar should seek to enjoin the nonattorney's activities or if the nonattorney should be referred to a state attorney for prosecution. To enjoin the nonattorney, the Florida Bar files a petition with the Florida Supreme Court.

In the first half of 1995, the Florida Bar added unlicensed practice of law investigators in Orlando, Tampa, and Miami and opened 300 new cases, including 120 cases in the central Florida area. "The bar has sought recent Supreme Court injunctions against a former Orange County man convicted of bilking eight clients for $13,000 in services he didn't perform, a former Winter Park woman who acted as legal representative for a friend and an Orlando company whose salesmen sold people living trusts they may not have needed."[79]

This expansion in the Florida Bar's Unlicensed Practice of Law Department resulted in a dramatic increase in the number of unlicensed practice of law complaints and a decrease in the average time period necessary to resolve the complaints. In the early 1990s there were approximately 275 new unlicensed practice-of-law complaints annually. The number of new complaints increased to 700 by 1999, with an annual average of 640 complaints and inquiries by the end of 2006. In 1998, the average unlicensed practice of law case lasted 272 days, a substantial decrease from the 1994 average of 826. In 2002, the bar closed 782 cases, ninety-two ending in an injunction, twenty-four with cease and desist affidavits, and several with contempt citations. At the close of 2006, fifty-one unauthorized practice of law lawsuits were pending.[80]

Typically the bar requests cease and desist affidavits from those engaged in the unauthorized practice of law. If the violation continues, the bar obtains an injunction from the Florida Supreme Court and may request that the violator be held in indirect criminal contempt, with a jail term of up to five months, for breach of the injunction.[81] In 2005, the Florida Supreme Court enjoined fourteen individuals and businesses from the unauthorized practice of law.[82]

For the most serious unauthorized practice of law cases, the bar has the option of prosecuting an individual for indirect criminal contempt without the Florida Supreme Court issuing an injunction. The procedure for instituting indirect contempt proceedings is detailed in the Rules Regulating the Florida Bar. Prior to prosecution, the bar must receive approval from the standing committee and the Board of Governors. Then the Florida Bar files a petition with the Florida Supreme Court requesting a contempt citation. The Florida Supreme Court's order to show cause directs the individual to appear before a referee for arraignment. If the individual pleads not guilty, the bar must prove the individual's guilt beyond a reasonable doubt at a hearing before the referee. The referee finds the individual guilty or not guilty and, if guilty, forwards the finding to the Florida Supreme Court together with the recommended sentence. The Florida Supreme Court is free to approve, modify, or reject the referee's recommendation. The Florida Supreme Court may impose a prison sentence of up to five months or a fine of up to $2,500, or both.[83]

Over the last few years, the Florida Supreme Court imposed prison sentences for indirect criminal contempt, with some individuals' sentences suspended on the condition that they refrain from the unauthorized practice of law.[84]

In a case from 1994, a father and daughter had set up a "Constitutional Court of We The People In and For the United States of America" and "granted divorces, decided property disputes and issued 'warrants' against real judges." The Florida Supreme Court enjoined the couple, and the Florida Bar filed a petition in the Florida Supreme Court to have them held in contempt when they did not stop their activities.[85]

In 1998, after being convicted of six counts of unlicensed practice of
law, Jesse Toca was sentenced to two years in prison and four years
probation. Toca had been hired by individuals facing foreclosure on
their property; he used a number of tactics to delay the foreclosures.
Among other actions, Toca helped the individuals file fraudulent
bankruptcy petitions, notices removing cases to federal court, motions
to recuse the presiding judges, and quitclaim deeds on the disputed
property. These activities were successful in stretching a three- to six-
month foreclosure into several years and forcing some foreclosure
plaintiffs to abandon their claims.[86]

In 2001, the Florida Supreme Court enjoined Jorge Miguel Fernandez
from practicing law without a license and ordered him to make
restitution payments for legal fees paid him by his victims. Fernandez
never made the payments and left the country. Florida Department of
Law Enforcement agents arrested him at Miami International Airport
on March 10, 2004, on a Racketeer Influenced Corrupt Organization
charge of allegedly defrauding at least thirty-seven people in central
and south Florida between February and September 2001. Each
victim paid Fernandez's company $150 to $700 for legal services.
Prior to the 2001 injunction against him, victims who believed
Fernandez to be an attorney had filed thirteen complaints against
Fernandez with the Florida Bar.[87]

In March 2005 the Florida Supreme Court ordered that Michael
Bowers of Pensacola be incarcerated for five months for violating the
court's order against engaging in the unauthorized practice of law.
The court had enjoined Bowers from practicing law without a license
in 1998, and in 2002 had held Bowers in contempt for violating the
injunction. Although the court suspended Bowers's sentence and
placed him on probation in 2002, Bowers continued to practice law.[88]

Florida Court System

Article V of the Florida Constitution, effective January 1, 1973,
greatly simplified the Florida court system. The court system
comprises only four courts: the **Florida Supreme Court**, the
district courts of appeal, the **circuit courts**, and the **county
courts**. The Florida constitution prohibits the establishment of any
other courts but allows all courts, except for the Florida Supreme
Court, to sit in divisions.[89] The circuit and county courts have civil

and criminal divisions. In addition, the circuit court has probate and family law divisions (also referred to in some circuits as domestic relations division). **Small claims court** and **traffic court** are divisions of the county courts.[90] Figure 1 shows the structure of the Florida court system.

The Florida court system is composed of **trial courts** and **appellate courts**. Trial courts include Florida county courts and circuit courts. If there is a **jury trial**, the jury determines the **facts** and the judge rules on **questions of law**. If there is a **bench trial** (nonjury trial), the judge both determines the facts and rules on questions of law.

Trial and appellate courts

Generally, the losing party may appeal the case to the next highest court. The decision of the lower court is presumed to be correct until the appellant shows **reversible error**. An appellate court may not **substitute its judgment** for that of the finder of fact (a jury in a jury trial and the judge in a nonjury trial) if the finding of fact was supported by **competent evidence**.[91] A discretionary act of the trial court will not be reversed unless the court **abused its discretion**. An appellate court may reverse a ruling on a question of law if the ruling was **erroneous**.[92]

Appellate courts include the circuit court (handling appeals from the county courts), the district courts of appeal, and the Florida Supreme Court. Generally, the district courts of appeal hear appeals from the circuit courts and the Florida Supreme Court hears appeals from the district courts of appeal.[93] Special matters, such as final judgments imposing the death penalty, may be appealed directly from the circuit court to the Florida Supreme Court. The Florida Supreme Court, the district courts of appeal, and the circuit courts have **original jurisdiction** to issue the following writs:[94]

Figure 1

Florida Court System
Florida Supreme Court
District Courts of Appeal
Circuit Courts   **Divisions of Circuit Court:** civil / criminal / family law / Probate
County Courts   **Divisions of County Courts:** civil / criminal / traffic / small claims

∞   **writ of prohibition** to prevent an action,
∞   **writ of mandamus** to compel performance of a public duty that the petitioner has a right to have performed,
∞   **writ of *quo warranto*** to determine by what authority one holds office or presumes to act, and
∞   **writ of habeas corpus** to obtain the release of any person allegedly wrongfully deprived of liberty.

Criminal and civil cases

Cases are either **criminal cases** or **civil cases**. The basis of a criminal case is an offense punishable by a governmental body. In contrast, a civil case is brought by a private individual to enforce a private right.

"**Crime**" includes felonies and misdemeanors. A **felony** is punishable by death or imprisonment. A felony is classified as capital felony, a life felony, a felony of the first degree, a felony of the second degree, and a felony of the third degree, depending on the severity. A **misdemeanor** is punishable by imprisonment in a county correctional facility for not more than a year. A misdemeanor is classified as a misdemeanor of the first degree and a misdemeanor of the second degree, depending on the severity. Except for a capital felony, a fine may be imposed instead of or in addition to any prison term.[95]

The Florida constitution guarantees the defendant in a criminal case a **"speedy and public trial by impartial jury**."[96] Generally, misdemeanors must be brought to trial within ninety days after the defendant is taken into custody, and felonies must be brought to trial within 175 days.[97]

The Florida constitution guarantees "[a]ccess to courts . . . to every person for redress of any injury."[98] Matters commonly dealt with in civil cases include **contracts** and torts. If you had performed work under a contract but the other party to the contract refused to pay you, you might file a civil action or case to enforce the contract (get the other person to pay you). A **tort** involves an injury to a person or to property caused intentionally or through someone's negligence. Usually the **plaintiff** (the person who filed the lawsuit) is suing for money damages to compensate the plaintiff for a loss. Sometimes in a civil case the plaintiff is requesting an **injunction** or other relief such as **specific performance**. An injunction is a court order prohibiting or commanding some action. Specific performance is a court order compelling a party to comply with a contract. For example, if someone has a contract to purchase a house, but the seller refuses to complete the sale, the buyer may be able to obtain a court order of specific performance ordering the seller to complete the sale. Other civil matters include adoption, change of name, dissolution of marriage, **probate** (review of wills and distribution of a decedent's property), and traffic infractions. An **infraction** is a noncriminal violation punishable by fine rather than prison.[99]

The costs may be waived if a person is unable to pay court costs and files an affidavit stating that "I am presently unable to pay court costs and fees. Under penalty of perjury, I swear or affirm that all statements in this affidavit are true and complete."[100]

Venue

Venue is the geographical location in which a case has been filed.

Venue of a Civil Case

The plaintiff may file a case in either of the following locations:

∞   If the defendant is an individual, where the defendant lives, or if
     a corporation, in the county in which the corporation's office is
     located. (With multiple defendants living in different counties,
     the case may be filed in a county in which a defendant lives.)
∞   Where the case **accrued** (developed).[101]

Where the case accrued depends on the type of case:

∞   If the case is based on an injury or accident, it is the place the
     injury or accident occurred.
∞   If the case is based on a contract, it is the place the contract was
     breached. As an alternative, the parties can agree where a case is
     to be filed in the event of breach.[102] A **forum selection** clause
     will be enforced unless it is unreasonable or unjust.[103]
∞   If the case is based on a promissory note, it is the county in
     which the note was signed.[104]
∞   If the case is based on litigation involving real property, it is
     where the property is located.[105]

A **change of venue** (moving the case from one county court to
another, or from one circuit court to another) may be granted for the
following reasons:

∞   if the case was filed in the improper court.
∞   if one party will not receive a fair trial either because the other
     party "has an undue influence over the minds of the inhabitants
     of the county" or one party "is so odious to the inhabitants of the
     county that he or she could not receive a fair trial."
∞   if "it appears impracticable to obtain a qualified jury in the
     county" in which the case was filed.
∞   "[f]or the convenience of the parties or witnesses or in the
     interest of justice."[106]

Venue of a Criminal Case

Venue of a criminal case is the county in which the crime was committed.[107] The venue of a criminal case may be changed "on the ground that a fair and impartial trial cannot be had in the county where the case is pending for any reason other than the interest and prejudice of the trial judge."[108]

Florida County Courts

Jurisdiction

According to the Florida constitution, each of the sixty-seven counties in Florida has a county court.[109] The county courts have jurisdiction

∞ of all **misdemeanors** not handled by the circuit courts.

∞ of all **violations of city and county ordinances.**

∞ of all actions in which the amount in controversy (not including attorney's fees and costs) **does not exceed $15,000**, except those handled by the circuit court.

∞ concurrent with the circuit court, of **landlord-tenant** cases not exceeding $15,000.

∞ of matters concerning the right to possession of real property and to the forcible or unlawful detention of any interest in real property (except jurisdiction is concurrent with the circuit court if the amount in controversy is more than $15,000 or the circuit otherwise has jurisdiction).

In addition, the county court may hear dissolution of marriage cases under the simplified dissolution procedure or may issue a dissolution of marriage in an uncontested case.[110]

The Florida Supreme Court prepares an annual report for each fiscal year. The annual report contains the number of case filings by county and division for the fiscal year as well as a historical comparison with the number of filings in prior years. Annual reports are accessible through the Florida State Courts website at http://www.flcourts.org/.

Procedure

For procedure (other than cases in small claims court and traffic court), see "Procedure" (under "Florida Circuit Courts") on page 27.

Judges

The Florida Legislature sets the number of judges for the county courts. In 2006, the number of county judges ranged from one for the thirty-three least populous counties, to seventeen for Duval County (Jacksonville), to eighteen for Orange County (Orlando), to fifteen for Hillsborough County (Tampa), to seventeen for Pinellas County (St. Petersburg), to nineteen for Palm Beach County, to thirty-two for Broward County, to forty-three for Dade County (Miami).[111] County court judges may be assigned to divisions within the court. For example, of the eighteen county court judges in Orange County in 2007, four were assigned to the civil division, ten were assigned to the criminal division, and four were assigned to the jail.

County court judges must have been members of the Florida Bar for five years, except in counties with a population not exceeding 40,000. In counties with a population of 40,000 or less, a county court judge must be a member of the Florida Bar or have completed a law training program. (An exception is made for one who is already a county court judge, so long as the judge is not under suspension or disqualification.) The mandatory retirement age is seventy, except that if one-half of a term has been completed when the judge turns seventy, the rest of the term may be completed.[112] County court judges are required to be full-time judges and may not practice law or hold political office in any political party.[113]

County court judges have six-year terms. Beginning with the 2000 general election, a majority of the voters within the county may decide to select county court judges by merit selection and retention rather than by election. Should the county not vote for merit selection and retention, the county must wait at least two years to bring the matter to a vote again. Those counties not using merit selection and retention elect county court judges. In those counties with merit selection and retention, a county court judge who desires to serve a succeeding six-year term must **qualify for retention** by a vote of a majority of qualified voters within the county voting to retain.[114] If a vacancy occurs at any time during the six-year term and at the end of the six-year term for those counties using merit selection and retention, the governor may fill it from at least three persons nominated by a judicial nominating commission.[115] All county court judges are members of the **Conference of County Court Judges of Florida**. The conference meets annually and makes recommendations concerning improvement of the Florida judicial system and court procedure. The conference also presents continuing judicial education programs.[116]

Small Claims Court

Small claims court is a division of county court that handles civil cases if the amount in controversy is $5,000 or less, excluding costs, interest, and attorney's fees.[117] Generally the procedures followed in small claims court are less formal than in other civil trial courts. The Small Claims Rules generally dictate procedure but do make certain of the Rules of Civil Procedure applicable.[118] The Florida Evidence Code applies but is "to be liberally construed."[119]

A case in small claims court is begun by the plaintiff filing a **statement of claim**. At the plaintiff's request, the clerk's office may help in preparing the statement of claim. The court informs the parties of the date and time of the initial hearing of the case.[120] In the notice, the defendant is informed of the defendant's right of venue.[121]

"The law gives the person or company who has sued you the right to file suit in any one of several places as listed below. However, if you have been sued in any place other than one of these places, you, as the defendant, have the right to request that the case be moved to a proper location or venue. A proper location or venue may be one of the following:

- ∞ "where the contract was entered into"
- ∞ "if the suit is on an unsecured promissory note, where the note is signed or where the maker resides"
- ∞ "if the suit is to recover property or to foreclose a lien, where the property is located"
- ∞ "where the event giving rise to the suit occurred"
- ∞ "where any one or more of the defendants sued reside"
- ∞ "any location agreed to in a contract"

∞ "in an action for money due, if there is no agreement as to where suit may be filed, where payment is to be made."

The initial hearing of the case is also the **pretrial conference**. The pretrial conference is a meeting of the judge and the parties in preparation for trial. The trial is set not more than sixty days after the pretrial conference.[122]

Traffic Court

Traffic court is a division of county court that handles two types of traffic cases: **criminal traffic offenses** and **civil traffic infractions**.[123] The Rules of Criminal Procedure are applicable to the trial of criminal traffic offenses, except as provided in the **Rules of Traffic Court**.[124] County court judges preside over criminal traffic offenses.[125]

Unless a mandatory hearing on a civil traffic infraction is required, one may generally **waive** a hearing and may either pay a fine at the **traffic violations bureau** or may attend a **basic driver improvement course**.[126] If one elects to have a hearing, the infraction must be proved to have been committed beyond a reasonable doubt.[127] Hearings on civil traffic infractions may be presided over by a county court judge or by a **civil traffic infraction hearing officer**[128] (sometimes referred to as a **magistrate**). For example, in 2007, there were six county court judges and four hearing officers in the traffic court division of the County Court for Orange County. Magistrates have the same power to decide civil traffic infractions, except they:

∞   may not hold anyone in contempt of court,
∞   may not hear a case involving injury, and
∞   may not hear a case involving a civil traffic infraction and a criminal traffic offense.

A defendant may request to be tried by a county court judge rather than by a magistrate. Magistrates must be members of the Florida Bar, must complete a forty-hour training program, and must complete four hours of continuing education annually.[129]

Florida Circuit Courts

Jurisdiction

Florida is divided into twenty circuits, each served by a **circuit court**.[130] *See* the Florida state courts website, http://www.flcourts.org/ for the distribution of Florida counties into circuits and a map of the twenty judicial circuits. Circuit courts have jurisdiction[131]

∞   of **appeals** from county courts, except for the following that proceed to district courts of appeal:
  o   orders or judgments of the county court **declaring a state statute or Florida constitutional provision invalid**
  o   orders or judgments of county court **certified to the district court of appeal to be of great public importance** and that are accepted by the district court of appeal for review
∞   of actions at law not handled by the county courts.
∞   of probate matters (settlement of estates, guardianship matters, involuntary hospitalization, competency hearings, etc.).
∞   generally, of **equity** matters (equitable relief is generally relief other than money damages, such as an injunction or specific performance).
∞   of all felonies and related misdemeanors.
∞   of cases concerning the legality of a tax assessment, toll, or denial of a refund.
∞   of ejectments.
∞   of actions concerning real property title and boundaries.
∞   to review administrative action, as provided by general law.

The Florida Supreme Court prepares an annual report for each fiscal year. The annual report contains the number of case filings by circuit, county, and division for the fiscal year as well as a historical comparison with the number of filings in prior years. Annual reports are accessible through the Florida State Courts website at http://www.flcourts.org/.

Procedure

In a civil case, the only pleadings allowed are a(n)

- ∞ **complaint** (in some types of cases referred to as a **petition**)— the first pleading in a case which the plaintiff states the plaintiff's claim or right to file the case and the relief requested.
- ∞ **answer**—the response to the complaint or petition, which may contain a counterclaim, a crossclaim, or an affirmative defense.
- ∞ **answer** to a **counterclaim** (a claim of the defendant against the plaintiff).
- ∞ **answer** to a **crossclaim** (a counterclaim against another defendant or another plaintiff).
- ∞ **third-party complaint**—a complaint filed by a defendant against a third party, claiming that the third party is liable to the defendant.
- ∞ **third-party answer**—answer of the third party.
- ∞ **reply** to an **affirmative defense**—an affirmative defense is a defense raised by the defendant, which, if proved, could hold the plaintiff liable.[132]

All pleadings and other documents filed by an attorney must be signed by an attorney in the attorney's name and must state the attorney's address, telephone number with area code, and Florida Bar number. Pleadings generally do not need to be **verified**.[133] A verification contains a sworn statement that the facts in the pleading are true. All documents filed must be on 8½-by-11-inch recycled paper, but exhibits or attachments may be in their original size.[134]

Judges

The Florida Legislature sets the number of judges per circuit. In 2006, the number of judges per circuit ranged from four to eighty.[135] A circuit court judge must have been a member of the Florida Bar for five years. Circuit court judges have six-year terms.[136] Beginning with the 2000 general election, a majority of the voters within the circuit may decide to select circuit court judges by merit selection and retention rather than by election. Should voters within the circuit not vote for merit selection and retention, the circuit must wait at least two years to bring the matter to a vote again. Those circuits not using merit selection and retention elect circuit court judges. In those circuits with merit selection and retention, a circuit court judge who desires to serve a succeeding six-year term must **qualify for retention** by a vote of a majority of qualified voters within the circuit voting to retain.[137] The mandatory retirement age is seventy, except that if one-half of a term has been completed when the judge turns seventy, the rest of the term may be completed.[138] Circuit judges are required to be full-time judges and may not practice law or hold political office in any political party.[139] The governor may fill a vacancy from at least three persons nominated by a judicial nominating commission. When the term of the appointed judge expires, the position is filled by election in those circuits not using merit selection and retention.[140] A county court judge who has been a member of the Florida Bar for at least five years may be temporarily assigned to preside over circuit court cases.[141]

A majority of the circuit and county judges within a circuit select one of the circuit judges to be the chief judge of the circuit. If there is no majority, the chief judge is selected by the chief justice. In addition to the regular responsibilities of a judge, the chief judge handles administrative matters for the circuit.[142] All active and retired circuit court judges are members of the **Conference of Circuit Judges of Florida**. The conference makes recommendations concerning improvement of the Florida judicial system and court procedure. Recommendations of the conference are reported to the Florida Supreme Court. In addition, recommendations for legislative action are reported to the president of the Florida Senate and the speaker of the Florida House not less than sixty days before the regular session of the Florida Legislature.[143]

Circuit judges are usually assigned to a division within the court. For example, in 2007, in the Circuit Court for Orange County, one judge was designated chief judge, eight judges were assigned to the **civil division**, twelve judges to the **criminal division**, seven judges to the **domestic relations division**, one judge to the **probate division**, and five judges to the **juvenile division**. Within the civil division, one of the judges of the civil division was appointed the **administrative judge**, with responsibility for "generally overseeing the operation and functioning of the civil division." Judges within the civil division are paired up. If an emergency matter arises and the judge assigned to a particular case is unable to handle the matter, the other judge in the pair, the **alternate judge**, handles the matter. Emergency matters arising other than during regular operating hours are handled by the **duty judge**, the judge on call to handle such matters.[144]

Magistrates

In 2004, the Florida Legislature funded circuit court magistrate programs. Magistrates hear matters upon referral from a judge and consent of the parties. After conducting a hearing, the magistrate files a report with the court, which may include findings of fact prior to trial, and serves copies of the report on the parties. The parties may make exception to the report within ten days of service upon them.[145]

Personnel

Each circuit court has a **clerk of the circuit court**.[146] The **county sheriff** is the executive officer of the circuit court of the county.[147] The plaintiff in a civil case begins the case by **filing** the complaint with the clerk and paying the applicable **filing fee**. Once a case has been filed, whether civil or criminal, the clerk keeps "a progress docket in which he or she shall note the filing of each pleading, motion, or other paper and any step taken by him or her in connection with each action, appeal, or other proceeding before the court" and an alphabetical index for the docket. **Orders of dismissal** (court decisions terminating a case) and **final judgments** (court decisions terminating the case on the merits) are **recorded** (made an official and public record) by the clerk.[148] The county sheriff has the power to execute service of process.[149]

The **official court reporter**, an employee of the court, reports the testimony and proceedings in preliminary hearings and trials of criminal cases and juvenile proceedings at public expense. The official court reporter may be assisted by deputy court reporters. If a court reporter is desired in a civil case, the attorney must request and pay for the services of a court reporter. The court reporter makes notes of the proceedings generally using a finger-operated machine or repeating the proceedings into a funnel-shaped recording device. In addition, proceedings may be taped. Upon request, the court reporter may furnish a typewritten **transcript**.[150]

Other court personnel may include **judicial assistants, trial clerks**, and **court deputies**.[151] Each judge usually has a judicial assistant, a trial clerk, and a court deputy (sometimes referred to as a bailiff). One law clerk may assist a number of judges. The judicial assistant assists the judge in administrative matters, including scheduling hearings and trials, organizing court files, and maintaining contact with attorneys. A trial clerk generally takes minutes of court proceedings and takes charge of exhibits. The court deputy maintains order in the courtroom. The law clerk, usually a recent law school graduate, performs legal research and may assist the judges in writing opinions or other court documents.

Family Division

In 1990, the Florida Legislature created the Commission on Family Courts to study the need for family courts. The commission reported its recommendations to the Florida Supreme Court. As a result, in September 1991, the Florida Supreme Court ruled that each circuit should establish a family division of the circuit court or should design a plan to coordinate single-family law matters. The goal of the Family Court Initiative was:

> To provide an integrated coordinated response to family members in need of court intervention so as to maximize the use of available court and community-based resources for the constructive, expeditious resolution of such matters. These matters shall include, but not be limited to: dissolution, child custody, and related domestic matters; juvenile dependency and delinquency; and domestic and repeat violence.[152]

The circuit-developed plans include various programs to help family members involved with the courts: case management units, domestic violence intake units, *pro se* assistance services, family mediation services, guardian *ad litem* programs, parent orientation courses, teen court, supervised visitation, and batterer's treatment programs.[153] Funds to implement the family court plans and hire administrative and support staff were generated from an increase in fees for marriage licenses.[154]

Case management units organize the handling of family law cases to move the cases through the court in an efficient manner.

Domestic violence intake units "may serve all or a combination of the following functions:

> dispensing information to parties, directing parties to
> the proper offices of the court, providing filing forms
> and petitions, assisting litigants in filling out forms,
> determining the type of filing required, and referring
> parties to appropriate court-sponsored or community-
> based service programs."[155]

Pro se assistance services provide services to help the person who does not have an attorney (the **pro se litigant**) navigate a family law case. Services provided include

> dispensing information to parties on petitions for
> divorce, custody, child support, modification, name
> change, and more; providing filing forms and
> petitions; assisting litigants in filling out forms; and
> referring parties to appropriate court-sponsored or
> community-based service programs.[156]

At least sixteen circuits have **family mediation programs** (for information on mediation, see "Mediation" on page 46). Several circuits have established dependency mediation programs and juvenile arbitration programs. A **dependency** case is one in which there are reasonable grounds to take the child into custody and removal is necessary to protect the child.[157] The dependency mediation programs provide an alternative to court proceedings. The **juvenile arbitration programs** "are designed to divert juveniles who have committed minor offenses from further involvement in the juvenile justice system. A juvenile who commits a crime can be referred to arbitration before going to court, with the approval of the state attorney." Available sanctions include

- ∞   restitution payment schedule,
- ∞   community service,
- ∞   jail tours,
- ∞   written apology to victim,
- ∞   restrictions and/or curfew, and
- ∞   other agreements between the victim and offender.[158]

All circuits have **guardian ad litem** programs. The programs appoint volunteers (guardians *ad litem*) to represent the best interests of children involved in juvenile, criminal, and family law cases.

Parent orientation courses, established in many circuits, educate divorcing parents on "the problems associated with divorce/custody/litigation, and assist them in helping their children cope with the divorce."[159]

Teen court "is run by teens for teens." Sentences are imposed by teen juries and are often composed of community service hours, essays, and service on future juries.

A number of circuits have **supervised visitation programs** that allow the noncustodial parent to visit the child in a controlled setting. The supervised visitation is used in custody, dependency, or domestic violence cases where there are "reasonable and serious concerns regarding the safety and well-being of children" involved. "These concerns may involve allegations of substance abuse, risk of abduction, physical or mental abuse, neglect, violence, or any serious physical or mental condition which would constitute a real and present danger to the child."[160]

Legislation passed in the 1995 session of the Florida Legislature requires attendance of an alleged batterer at a "**batterers' intervention program** as a condition of the [domestic violence] injunction, unless the court makes written factual findings in its judgment or order that are based on substantial evidence, stating why batterers' intervention programs would be inappropriate."[161]

In 2004, the Florida Legislature funded circuit court magistrate programs. Magistrates hear domestic relations matters (except for domestic, repeat, dating, and sexual violence) upon referral from a judge and consent of the parties.[162] Magistrates may also conduct mental health hearings[163] and can assist in juvenile dependency cases.[164]

Florida District Courts of Appeal

Jurisdiction

Florida is divided into five appellate districts, each served by a district court of appeal.[165] The following are the headquarters of the district courts of appeal[166]

∞   First District Court of Appeal—Tallahassee

∞   Second District Court of Appeal—Lakeland

∞   Third District Court of Appeal—Dade County

∞   Fourth District Court of Appeal—Palm Beach County

∞   Fifth District Court of Appeal—Daytona Beach

The district courts of appeal have jurisdiction[167]

∞   to hear appeals of trial court decisions that are not directly appealable to the circuit court or to the Florida Supreme Court.

∞   in accordance with applicable court rule, to review **interlocutory orders** (orders during the case that do not terminate the case).

∞   in accordance with general law, to review administrative action.

See the Florida state courts website, http://www.flcourts.org/, for the distribution of Florida state court circuits into districts and a map of the five judicial districts. The Florida Supreme Court prepares an annual report for each fiscal year. The annual report contains the number of case filings by district for the fiscal year as well as a historical comparison with the number of filings in prior years. Annual reports are accessible through the Florida State Courts website at http://www.flcourts.org/.

Procedure

On appeal, the court decides the case based on the **record**, the **briefs** filed, and any **oral argument**. The record generally comprises "the original documents, exhibits, and transcript(s) of proceedings, if any," of the lower court.[168] The briefs are the legal documents generally filed by the attorneys representing the parties on appeal. The types of briefs that may be filed are the "initial brief, the answer brief, a reply brief, and a cross-reply brief." The Florida Rules of Appellate Procedure specify the form and contents of briefs. The initial brief must contain

∞   a table of contents,
∞   a table of citations,
∞   a statement of the case and of the facts,
∞   a summary of the argument,
∞   the argument for each issue, and
∞   a conclusion containing the relief requested.[169]

Oral argument is a presentation of the case, usually by the attorneys for the parties, before the appellate judges designated to decide the case. Each party is allowed twenty minutes of oral argument, but in capital cases, each party is allowed thirty minutes.[170]

Except for **en banc** decisions, a **panel** of three judges considers each case, with the concurrence of a majority necessary to reach a decision.[171] In a "case of exceptional importance" or if "necessary to maintain uniformity in the court's decisions," a district court may hear a case *en banc*, that is, by all the district judges rather than by the usual three-judge panel. In other words, if a decision were heard *en banc* by the Fifth District Court of Appeal, all ten judges of the Fifth District Court of Appeal would hear the case. A case is heard *en banc* if a majority of the judges of the district court so order.[172]

Judges

The Florida Legislature sets the number of judges per appellate district. In 2006, the appellate districts had from ten to fifteen judges. The first district had fifteen, the second district had fourteen, the third district had eleven, the fourth district had twelve, and the fifth district had ten.[173] A district court judge must have been a member of the Florida Bar for ten years. The mandatory retirement age is seventy, except that if one-half of a term has been completed when the judge turns seventy, the rest of the term may be completed.[174] District court of appeal judges are required to be full-time judges and may not practice law or hold political office in any political party.[175] The governor appoints a judge to fill each vacancy, with the appointment made from no fewer than three persons nominated by a judicial nominating commission.[176] A judge who desires to serve a succeeding six-year term must **qualify for retention** by a vote of a majority of qualified voters within the geographical jurisdiction of the court voting to retain.[177] A majority of the members of the court of each district select one of the judges to be the chief judge of the district. If there is no majority, the chief judge is selected by the chief justice. In addition to the regular responsibilities of a district judge, the chief judge handles administrative matters for the district.[178]

Personnel

Each district court has a **clerk of the district court** and a **marshal**.[179] A petition invoking the original jurisdiction of the district court is begun by **filing** the petition with the clerk and paying the applicable **filing fee**. An appeal to the district court is begun by filing two copies of the **notice of appeal** with the lower court and paying the filing fee. The clerk of the lower court sends the filing fee and a copy of the notice of appeal to the district court. The clerk of the district court has custody of all case files and the original opinions of the district court.[180] Once a petition has been filed or a case appealed to the district court, the clerk's office keeps a progress docket noting the filing of each document and any action taken by the clerk's office concerning each case and an alphabetical index for the docket. The marshal has the power to execute service of process, is custodian of the headquarters of the district court, and is charged with keeping the peace at the headquarters of the district court. The marshal is required to complete a training program approved by the Criminal Justice Standards and Training Commission of the Department of Law Enforcement.[181]

Other court personnel may include **judicial assistants** (or secretaries), **staff attorneys** or **law clerks**, and **courtroom personnel**. Each judge usually has a judicial assistant and two staff attorneys or law clerks. The judicial assistant assists the judge in administrative matters. Staff attorneys and law clerks perform legal research and may assist the judges in writing opinions or other court documents.

Florida Supreme Court

Jurisdiction

In Florida, the **court of last resort** is the Florida Supreme Court, with headquarters in Tallahassee.[182] Its jurisdiction[183] is **mandatory** on a few matters, but otherwise it is **discretionary**. The Florida Supreme Court *must hear*

∞ appeals from trial court final judgments imposing the death penalty;

∞ district court of appeal decisions declaring a state statute or Florida constitutional provision invalid;

∞ when provided by general law, appeals from decisions concerning the validation of bonds or certificates of indebtedness;

∞ when provided by general law, action of statewide agencies relating to utility rates or services; and

∞ a request for an advisory opinion from the state attorney general.

The Florida Supreme Court *may review*

∞ a district court of appeal decision expressly declaring a state statute valid;

∞ a district court of appeal decision expressly interpreting a Florida or United States constitutional provision;

∞ a district court of appeal decision expressly affecting a class of constitutional or state officers;

∞ a district court of appeal decision expressly and directly conflicting on the same question of law with a decision of another district court or of the Supreme Court;

∞ a district court of appeal decision certifying a question to be of great public importance;

∞ a district court of appeal decision certifying a question to be in direct conflict with a decision of another district court;

∞ a trial court decision certified by the district court of appeal in an pending case to be of great public importance;

∞ a trial court decision certified by the district court of appeal in a pending case to have a great effect on the proper administration of justice statewide and certified to require immediate resolution; and

∞ a question of law certified by the United States Supreme Court or a United States Court of Appeals, determinative of the case and which has no Florida Supreme Court precedent.

In addition, the governor "may request in writing the opinion of the justices of the supreme court as to the interpretation of any portion of [the Florida] [C]onstitution upon any question affecting the governor's executive powers and duties"[184] and the attorney general must "request the opinion of the justices of the supreme court as to

the validity of any initiative petition" to amend the Florida
constitution.[185] Currently, the court spends 25 to 30 percent of its time
on death penalty appeals.[186] The Florida Supreme Court prepares an
annual report for each fiscal year. The annual report contains the
number of case filings for the Florida Supreme Court for the latest
fiscal year for which the information is available as well as a historical
comparison with the number of filings in prior years. Annual reports
are accessible through the Florida State Courts website at
http://www.flcourts.org/. In fiscal year 2004–2005 there were 2,475
cases filed in the Florida Supreme Court.

Procedure

The *Supreme Court Manual of Internal Operating Procedures*,
de-signed to "make the judicial process more comprehensible to the
general public," gives a glimpse of the way the court handles oral
argument.[187] The balance of this section contains provisions taken
from the manual.

∞ **"Preargument Procedures.** Oral arguments are routinely
scheduled for the first full week of each month, except that no
arguments are heard on state holidays or during the months of July
and August. When the case is scheduled for oral argument, the clerk's
office sends copies of the briefs to each justice. At least two months
before the first day of the month in which oral argument has been
scheduled, the case file goes to the office of the assigned justice. The
assigned justice's office summarizes and analyzes the issues raised in
the briefs in a memorandum for use on the bench and circulates it to
each justice no later than the Wednesday of the week preceding oral
argument. The director of public information prepares a brief
summary on each oral argument case, which is available to the public
a few days prior to oral argument and is posted on the Supreme Court
Press Page of the Court's website located at
http://www.floridasupremecourt.org/pub_ info/index.shtml. The
briefs are also posted here. These summaries are not official Court
documents."

∞ **"Oral Argument Procedures.** On oral argument days, counsel
appearing that day are required to sign in with the clerk's office
starting thirty minutes before arguments are scheduled to begin. At
this time coffee is available for counsel in the lawyers' lounge, and

the justices may join counsel for conversation not relating to cases
scheduled for argument."

"Oral argument routinely begins at 9:00 a.m., ET, but may be
scheduled by the chief justice to begin at other times. Oral argument
on Fridays begins at 8:30 a.m., ET. Approximately ten minutes
before arguments begin, the justices assemble in the robing room to
don their robes for the bench. At the time arguments are to begin, the
marshal announces that the Court is in session and the justices enter
the courtroom from behind the bench, led by the chief justice or
acting chief justice, in order of seniority. Retired justices or judges
assigned to temporary duty on the court enter last. Seating alternates
from right to left, based on seniority. All justices remain standing
until the chief justice indicates that all justices are in place.

"The chief justice controls the order of argument and the time
allowed to any party. The division of time for argument between co-
counsel or among multiple counsel on one side of a case, and
between counsel's main presentation and rebuttal, is solely counsel's
responsibility. In order to assist counsel, however, amber and red
lights are mounted on the lectern. When the chief justice recognizes
counsel, the allotted time begins. The amber light indicates that
counsel has either (1) entered the time requested to be set aside for
rebuttal, (2) gone into the time set aside for co-counsel's argument, or
(3) entered the period of time near the end of argument when notice
of the remaining time has been requested. The red light indicates that
counsel's allotted time has expired, at which point counsel will be
expected to relinquish the lectern. Any justice may ask questions or
make comments at any time. The chief justice has discretion to
authorize a recess during oral argument and by tradition has done so
midway into the calendar. During this mid-morning recess, the
justices will not meet with counsel.

"At the conclusion of the calendar, the Court is adjourned. The
justices leave the bench in the order they entered and reassemble in
the conference room for a preliminary conference on the cases
argued. No person may enter the conference room without the
invitation of the full court."

∞   "**Electronic Recording and Broadcasts.** The Court records
audiotapes of all oral arguments held in the courtroom. The

audiotapes are kept with the case file and are retained until the case has become final, that is, until any motion for rehearing has been disposed of by the Court. Audiotapes of arguments in capital cases, however, are retained indefinitely. Florida State University, through WFSU-TV, records all oral arguments on videotape, copies of which are available from WFSU-TV by calling (850) 487-3170 or (800) 322-WFSU. Except when preempted by legislative sessions, oral arguments are broadcast live via the AMC-3 satellite, KU band, at 87 degrees west, transponder 18, virtual channel 802. The downlink frequency is 12046.750 MHz. The uplink frequency is 14348.500 MHz. The L-band frequency is 1296.750 MHz. The symbol rate is 7.32. The FEC is 3/4. The satellite may be preempted during legislative sessions and emergencies. Oral arguments are broadcast live on the Florida channel, which is available statewide at the discretion of local cable providers. Arguments also are broadcast worldwide on the Internet in RealPlayer video and audio formats from a website jointly maintained with WFSU-TV (http://wfsu.org/gavel2gavel/). An archive of RealPlayer video and audio from previous arguments is maintained on the same website. The Court calendar, briefs, press summaries, and other information about cases and about using the Internet are posted on the Supreme Court Public Information Page of the Court's website located at http://www.floridasupremecourt.org/pub_info/index.shtml."

∞ **"Recusals.** On occasion, a justice will elect to recuse himself or herself from a particular case for good cause. A justice thus recused from any case set for oral argument notifies the chief justice in advance of argument. If four of the remaining justices cannot ultimately agree to a disposition, the chief justice assigns a judge, senior judge, or senior justice to the case. As a general rule, in such instance, reargument on the case will not be scheduled, because video and audio of the argument will be made available to the assigned judge, senior judge, or senior justice.

"After oral argument, the justices confer and take a tentative vote on the cases argued. The author of the Court's opinion or disposition is ordinarily the assigned justice, and the case file is sent to that justice after conference. Once an opinion has been written, a facing vote sheet is attached in the author's office, and the opinion, the vote sheet, and case file are delivered to the clerk's office.

"The assigned justice's office electronically distributes copies to each justice. Each justice votes electronically, making any comments deemed appropriate. If a concurring or dissenting opinion is written, that opinion and its vote sheet are also delivered to the clerk, and the authoring justice's office electronically distributes copies of these papers to the other justices. When all justices have voted on all the separate opinions in a case, the clerk's office determines if a panel has four concurring votes. If not, the case is scheduled for discussion at the next regularly scheduled conference in order to reconcile the disparate views. If any justice has requested that the case be discussed at conference, the case is placed on the conference schedule.

"When the clerk's office determines that a case has the necessary votes for release, the case is then sent to the reporter of decisions for technical review. The reporter of decisions then directs the clerk in writing to file as an opinion of the Court any opinion to which four justices subscribe.

"Copies of opinions ready for release to the public are delivered to each justice not later than Friday at noon. At any time before 10 a.m., ET, the following Thursday, any justice may direct the clerk not to release an opinion. Unless otherwise directed, on Thursday morning at 11 a.m. the clerk electronically releases the opinions furnished to the justices the preceding Friday. Publishers other than the Court's official reporter may receive copies at the rate of fifty cents per page, and all other interested persons may receive copies at the cost of one dollar per page. Opinions are posted on the Opinions and Rules Page of the court's website located at http://www.floridasupremecourt.org/decisions/index.shtml by noon on the day they are released. . . . Opinions may be released at any other time at the direction of the chief justice. When opinions are released at other times, the director of public information notifies news media as soon as is practicable."[188]

Justices

The Florida Supreme Court is made up of seven justices, with each appellate district having at least one justice who was a resident of the district at the time the justice joined the court. A justice must have been a member of the Florida Bar for ten years. The mandatory retirement age is seventy, except that if one-half of a term has been completed when the justice turns seventy, the rest of the term may be completed.[189] Justices are required to serve full-time and may not practice law or hold political office in any political party.[190] The governor appoints a justice to fill each vacancy, with the appointment made from no fewer than three nor more than six persons nominated by a **judicial nominating commission**.[191] A justice who desires to serve a succeeding six-year term must **qualify for retention** by obtaining the vote of a majority of qualified voters within the geographical jurisdiction of the court.[192] Five justices are necessary for a quorum. At least four justices are necessary to render a decision.[193] A majority of court members select one of the justices to be the chief justice. The chief justice serves as the chief administrative officer of the Florida judicial system in addition to bearing the regular responsibilities of a justice.[194]

Personnel

The **staff of the chief justice** includes an **executive assistant**, two **staff attorneys**, four **judicial assistants**, an **inspector general**, a **director of public information**, a **central staff of attorneys**, and a **reporter of decisions**. The staff of each of the other justices includes three staff attorneys and a judicial assistant. Other court personnel include the **clerk of the Supreme Court**, the **marshal of the Supreme Court**, the **librarian of the Supreme Court**, and the **state courts administrator**. The clerk's office receives, organizes, and safeguards all documents and other papers filed with the court. The marshal executes process (gives legal notice of a court proceeding) and maintains the furnishing and grounds of the Florida Supreme Court building. The librarian is in charge of the Supreme Court Library, which is open to court personnel and to the public. The State Courts Administrator assists the chief justice in administrative matters concerning the Florida court system.[195]

Judicial Management Council of Florida

The **Judicial Management Council of Florida** is composed of a justice of the Florida Supreme Court, district court of appeal judges, circuit judges, county court judges, a state attorney, a public defender, the attorney general or designee, a clerk of the court, members of the Florida Bar, members of the public, members of the Florida Legislature, a member of the governor's legal staff, and a member of the Florida Council of 100. The principal responsibilities of the Judicial Management Council include:

∞ reviewing the organization and operation of the Florida court system,
∞ developing a strategic plan and a quality management and accountability program for the judicial branch, and
∞ recommending changes to the Constitutional Revision Commissions.

The council files an annual report with the Florida Supreme Court.[196]

Nomination, Discipline, and Removal of Judges

Nomination

The governor fills all vacancies on the Florida Supreme Court, the district courts of appeal, and those trial courts selecting judges by merit selection and retention from persons nominated by judicial nominating commissions. The same nomination and appointment procedure is followed to fill the unexpired term of an elected circuit or county court judge. Nominations are generally made within thirty days of the date on which the vacancy occurred, and the governor has sixty days to fill the vacancy.[197]

There are three levels of judicial nominating commissions. The **Supreme Court Judicial Nominating Commission** makes nominations for any Florida Supreme Court vacancy and the **District Courts of Appeal Judicial Nominating Commissions**, and the **Circuit Judicial Nominating Commissions** fill the same role for the district courts of appeal and the trial courts. There is one District Court of Appeal Judicial Nominating Commission for each of the five district courts of appeal and one circuit judicial nominating commission for each of the twenty circuits. The commissions review applications and interview a number of applicants. At the end of their investigation, the commissions select three nominees for each vacancy and forward the names of the nominees and investigative information to the governor.[198]

Discipline and Removal

The **Judicial Qualifications Commission** is in charge of investigating actions of Florida judges and justices, which may result in their discipline or removal. The commission is made up of two judges of the district courts of appeal, two judges of the circuit courts, two judges of the county courts, four members of the Florida Bar, and five members of the public. The commission receives information and decides whether formal charges should be filed against the judge or justice. The proceedings of the commission are confidential until formal charges are filed. After formal charges are filed, the commission holds a public hearing on the charges. At the conclusion of the hearing, the commission may recommend to the Florida Supreme Court discipline or removal upon vote of two-thirds of the members of the commission. Discipline or removal may be based on

> willful or persistent failure to perform judicial duties
> or for other conduct unbecoming a member of the
> judiciary demonstrating a present unfitness to hold
> office, or be involuntarily retired for any permanent
> disability that seriously interferes with the
> performance of judicial duties. Malafides [bad faith],
> scienter [knowledge of unfitness] or moral turpitude
> [depraved or immoral conduct] on the part of a justice
> or judge shall not be required for removal from office
> of a justice or judge whose conduct demonstrates a
> present unfitness to hold office.[199]

The Florida Supreme Court reviews the commission's recommendation in accordance with the Florida Rules of Appellate Procedure.[200]

On May 13, 2004, the Florida Supreme Court ordered that Judge Robert Lance Andrews, a circuit court judge of the seventeenth circuit, be publicly reprimanded for comments he made to a reporter concerning Novartis, a drug company who was a party to a lawsuit over which Judge Lance was presiding. The comments were that:

> 1. Novartis was trying to bury the plaintiffs in
> documents;

> 2. Novartis has only itself to blame for developments
> in the litigation;

> 3. The defense's strategy backfired; and

> 4. The entire database [the Special Master is creating at Novartis Pharmaceuticals' expense] would provide a national plaintiff's blueprint for filing suit against Novartis over Parlodel [the drug in the case.][201]

On December 7, 2006, the Florida Supreme Court removed Seminole County Court Judge Sloop for misconduct, including arresting eleven individuals who failed to attend a traffic court hearing before Judge Sloop because they had been directed to the wrong courtroom. The eleven were handcuffed, strip-searched, and incarcerated for nine hours. That incident followed Judicial Qualifications Commission investigations of Judge Sloop in 1991 and 2002. In rejecting the hearing panel's recommendation of a public reprimand and a ninety-day suspension, the Florida Supreme Court stated that it was "unconvinced that Judge Sloop can both effectively manage his temper and remain an effective jurist."[202]

The justices of the Florida Supreme Court and the judges of the district courts of appeal, the circuit courts, and the county courts may be **impeached** for "misdemeanor in office." A justice or judge is impeached upon two-thirds vote of the Florida House of Representatives and is tried by the Florida Senate. The trial must be held within six months of the impeachment. A justice or judge is convicted upon two-thirds vote of the Senate members present. The chief justice of the Florida Supreme Court, or another designated justice, presides at the trial, except that the governor presides at any trial of the chief justice.[203]

Alternative Dispute Resolution

Litigation (filing and pursuing lawsuits) is costly and time consuming. Some alternatives to litigation (**alternative dispute resolution**) are mediation, arbitration, and the use of Citizen Dispute Settlement Centers.

Mediation[204]

> means a process whereby a neutral third person called a mediator acts to encourage and facilitate the resolution of a dispute between two or more parties. It

is an informal and nonadversarial process with the
objective of helping the disputing parties reach a
mutually acceptable and voluntary agreement. In
mediation, decision-making authority rests with the
parties. The role of the mediator includes, but is not
limited to, assisting the parties in identifying issues,
fostering joint problem solving, and exploring
settlement alternatives [ways to end a dispute with
agreement].

Arbitration is "a process whereby a neutral third person or panel
considers the facts and arguments presented by the parties and renders
a decision which may be binding or nonbinding."[205] This contrasts
with mediation, in which the mediator helps the parties, but the parties
make any decision. Arbitration may be **binding** or **nonbinding**.[206] In
binding arbitration, the parties are required to comply with the
decision of the **arbitrator**(s), while in nonbinding arbitration, the
parties may, but are not required to, comply with the decision of the
arbitrator(s). A **citizen dispute settlement center** is "an informal
forum for the mediation and settlement of disputes."[207] Thus,
submitting a dispute to a citizen dispute settlement center is similar to
submitting a dispute to mediation. The proceeding in a citizen dispute
settlement center is more informal than that of mediation and may be
less costly.

Mediation

Since 1987, courts have been allowed to refer any civil lawsuit to
mediation. The practice of trial courts is to refer the bulk of the civil
cases to mediation. The local rules of the civil division of the Circuit
Court of Orange County, Florida, state, "[e]xcept where prohibited by
statute, mediation will be ordered in all cases where jury trial is
requested and in selected cases which are to be tried non-jury."[208]

Once a case is referred to mediation, the parties may select a mediator
within ten days. If the parties do not select a mediator, the court
appoints one. The first mediation conference is to be held within sixty
days of the order referring the case to mediation and the mediation is
generally to be completed within forty-five days of the first mediation
conference (seventy-five days for family mediation). The mediation
may result in an **agreement**, which is to be written and signed by the
parties and their attorneys, or **no agreement**. If the parties reach an

agreement, but the agreement is **breached** (not carried out), the court may impose **sanctions** (penalties), including ordering the breaching party to pay court costs and attorney's fees, or the court may enter judgment on the agreement.[209]

Mediators include **County Court Mediators, Family Mediators**, and **Circuit Court Mediators**. Mediators must meet the qualifications of the chief justice's administrative order.

Mediators must comply with the **Florida Rules for Certified and Court-Appointed Mediators**. A violation of the rules may result in the mediator being disciplined. Discipline ranges from requiring the mediator to pay the costs of a disciplinary hearing, to oral admonishment, to written reprimand, to suspension, to decertification.[210]

Arbitration

A dispute reaches arbitration in one of three ways:[211]

∞ a contract provision requires the parties to submit any dispute to binding arbitration,
∞ the parties to a dispute agree to submit the dispute to binding arbitration, or
∞ a judge orders the parties to submit the dispute to nonbinding arbitration.

Except as otherwise agreed to by the parties, each arbitrator must be a member of the Florida Bar, the chief arbitrator must have been a member of the Florida Bar for at least five years, and each arbitrator must have attended four hours of Florida Supreme Court–approved training.[212] Generally, arbitration sessions are scheduled with the American Arbitration Association, by the local bar association, or by another local entity. Submitting a dispute to arbitration results in a quicker decision than waiting for a decision in a lawsuit because of the congested court dockets. Arbitration may be less costly in a dispute involving a fairly large amount of money, but it may be more costly than a dispute involving a smaller amount of money that could be handled in small claims court.

In court-ordered arbitration, a written decision is made within ten days of the completion of the arbitration. A party to the arbitration may move for a trial by the court within twenty days after the parties are served with the arbitration decision. If no **trial *de novo*** (retrial) is requested, the judge enters any order or judgment required to enforce the arbitration decision.[213]

If the arbitration is binding, the arbitrator makes a written decision within ten days of the completion of the arbitration. A party to the arbitration may appeal the arbitration decision within thirty days after the parties are served with the arbitration decision. The only matters appealable are

∞ "any alleged failure of the arbitrators to comply with the applicable rules of procedure or evidence"
∞ "any alleged partiality or misconduct by an arbitrator prejudicing the rights of any party"
∞ "whether the decision reaches a result contrary to the Constitution of the United States or of the State of Florida."[214]

If no appeal is filed, the judge enters any order or judgment required to enforce the arbitration decision.[215]

Citizen Dispute Settlement Centers

A 1985 Florida statute allows the establishment of citizen dispute settlement centers. Each center is established locally and operates under a plan that details the procedure for scheduling mediation sessions, for giving notice of the time and place of the mediation session, and for conducting mediation. A mediator is immune from civil liability for actions taken as a mediator "unless such person acted in bad faith or with malicious purpose or in a manner exhibiting wanton and willful disregard of the rights, safety, or property of another."[216]

Let's look closer at the operations of a citizen dispute settlement center in Orange County, Florida. Although the statute authorizing the establishment of citizen dispute settlement centers dates from 1985, some citizen dispute settlement centers, like the citizen dispute settlement center of the Orange County Bar Association, were established before 1985. Established in 1975, the citizen dispute settlement center of the Orange County Bar Association operates out of the Orange County Bar Association offices. The types of disputes handled by the center include landlord-tenant, neighborhood disputes, property damage, recovery of money or property, animal nuisance, harassment, disorderly conduct, and consumer complaints.[217]

Once a mediation session is scheduled by one of the parties, letters are sent out to the parties notifying them of the time and place of the scheduled mediation and giving them information on the center. Local attorneys, members of the Orange County Bar Association, act as mediators. The attorneys donate their time as part of their annual **pro bono publico** obligation required to be a member of the Orange County Bar Association. *Pro bono publico* means "for the public good." An attorney performing services without being paid is working *pro bono*. There is no fee for the parties to attend the mediation session.

Florida Legal Research

Someone beginning to study law may be wondering what legal research has to do with law. After all, one doesn't see television and movie lawyers performing legal research or writing legal documents. They are usually portrayed arguing eloquently to the judge and jury. What television and movies don't show is all the legal research that took place before the lawyers entered the courtroom.

First, the lawyer has to know what the relevant law is before the lawyer can deal with the client's problem. Finding out what the law is requires legal research. Inadequate legal research or mistakes in written communication may cause problems for the client and may cause the lawyer to be disciplined or disbarred. Rule 4-1.1 of the Rules Regulating the Florida Bar, entitled "Competence," generally describes the type of representation the lawyer must provide the client. It states:

> A lawyer shall provide competent representation to a client. Competent representation requires the legal knowledge, skill, thoroughness, and preparation reasonably necessary for the representation.

The legal researcher must find all law relevant to the legal question being researched, must apply the law to the legal question, and must reach an answer. An answer to a legal question is inadequate if it is not supported by legal principles, if it is not based on current law, or if it is based on incomplete legal research. A lawyer's competency is immediately in question if the lawyer's argument does not take into account recent changes in the law or applicable legal principles.

The law library contains **primary sources, secondary sources**, and **finding tools**. Primary sources contain the law itself. Secondary sources contain commentary on the law. Finding tools are used to find primary and secondary sources. Primary sources, secondary sources, and finding sources used in researching Florida law are listed in Figure 2 on page 53.

If you are presently taking a legal research class, you may be using a nationally focused textbook as your main text in the class. For more information on legal research and research techniques, consult that text.

Primary sources

In legal writing, a statement about the law is usually supported by a citation to relevant primary sources. When a source is cited, its citation is given. A citation gives the location of the source so the reader can go to the law library and locate the source. If available, it is preferable to cite a primary source, rather than a secondary source commenting on a primary source. If there are no relevant primary sources, secondary sources may be cited. Finding tools are never cited or quoted. **Rule 9.800 of the Florida Rules of Appellate Procedure** is printed in Appendix A of this book. This rule gives the citation form to be used in documents submitted to Florida appellate courts. Notice that subsection (o) of the rule requires that material not covered by the rule be cited according to *The Bluebook: A Uniform System of Citation*. Until 2000, this publication, commonly referred to as the *Bluebook*, set the standard for proper legal citation. The ALWD Citation Manual published in 2000, with a second edition published in 2002, may become the new standard. The endnotes in this book are cited according to Rule 9.800 of the Florida Rules of Appellate Procedure.

Florida primary sources include the Florida constitution, cases, statutes, court rules, and administrative law. A chart showing the three branches of government and the names of primary sources produced by the branches is found in Figure 3 on page 55. Cases generally can be found in the law library in newsletter-type loose-leaf publications and in **reporters**. The Florida loose-leaf publication containing opinions of the Florida Supreme Court and the Florida district courts of appeal is ***Florida Law Weekly***. Some libraries that are government depositories may also have court opinions in **slip-opinion** form. Each opinion in slip-law form is published individually on the number of sheets of paper necessary to print the opinion.

"Reporters" are books containing court opinions. The reporter containing decisions of the Florida Supreme Court and the Florida district courts of appeal is ***Southern Reporter***. The volumes of reporters are numbered and the volumes are often printed in "series." Current Florida cases are found in *Southern Reporter, second series.* *Southern Reporter* contains decisions from Alabama, Florida, Louisiana, and Mississippi. To save on expense and shelf space, many Florida law libraries purchase the **Florida Cases** version of *Southern Reporter.* The Florida Cases version only contains cases originating in Florida, but the page numbering is the same as in the original version of *Southern Reporter.* A published Florida Supreme Court opinion would first be printed as a slip opinion and would then be published in *Florida Law Weekly.* The opinion would then be published in the paperbound version of *Southern Reporter* called **advance sheets**, followed by publication in *Southern Reporter.*

Southern Reporter, published by West Publishing Company, reports cases from 1887 to the present. Florida Supreme Court opinions from the first term of the court in 1846 through part of 1948 are reported in ***Florida Reports***. *Florida Reports* was the official reporter until it ceased publication. At that time, the Florida Supreme Court adopted *Southern Reporter* as Florida's official reporter.

Selected opinions of lower Florida courts and state commissions were printed in ***Florida Supplement*** and ***Florida Supplement, Second Series,*** from 1952 to July 1992. In July 1992 ***Florida Law Weekly Supplement***, a newsletter-type publication, began to print selected decisions of the Florida circuit and county courts and of state agencies.

Statutes are found in the law library in **session law** form, in **codes**, and in **annotated codes**. Some libraries that are government

depositories may also have statutes in **slip-law** form. Each statute in
slip-law form is published individually on the number of slips of
paper necessary to print the statute. When statutes are passed, they are
printed chronologically as session laws. Session laws are found in
West's *Florida Session Law Service* and ***Laws of Florida***.
West's *Florida Session Law Service* is a series of paperbound
pamphlets published during and soon after the end of the legislative
session. Laws of Florida is published in hardbound volumes in the
months following the legislative session's conclusion.

Florida statutes are codified (arranged by subject matter) in the
hardbound volume set called the **Florida Statutes**. *Florida Statutes*
is published at the end of the calendar year or at the beginning of the
following calendar year. For example, *Florida Statutes* 2008 is
published at the end of 2008 or at the beginning of 2009. The statutes
in *Florida Statutes* are divided into more than 1,000 chapters. These
chapters are further divided into sections. The statutes in *Florida
Statutes* are cited by decimal numbers, with the numbers to the left of
the decimal point

identifying the chapter number and the numbers following the
decimal point identifying the section number. In 1999, Florida made
the decision to recodify *Florida Statutes* every year. Previously,
Florida Statutes was recodified every odd-numbered year. Prior to
1999, a *Florida Statutes Supplement* was published in the even-
numbered years. The chapters are further divided into sections.

Figure 2

Primary Sources	Secondary Sources
Florida Constitution	*Florida Jurisprudence 2d*
Statutes	*American Law Reports*
∞ West's *Florida Session Law Service*	Law reviews
∞ *Florida Statutes*	Legal periodicals
∞ *Florida Statutes Annotated*	Treatises
∞ *Laws of Florida*	Continuing legal education publications
Loose-leaf service	**Finding Tools**
∞ *Florida Law Weekly*	
Reporters	*Florida Jurisprudence 2d*
∞ *Southern Reporter*	*American Law Reports*
∞ *Florida Law Weekly Supplement*	*Florida Digest 2d*
	Shepard's Florida Citations
	Shepard's Southern Citations
Administrative law	*Index to Legal Periodicals*
∞ *Florida Administrative Weekly*	
∞ *Florida Administrative Code*	
Florida court rules	

The supplement contained amended or new statutes passed during that year's legislative session.

Florida Statutes Annotated is a publication of West Group that contains the text of the statutes, with each statute followed by research material. This material includes notes on the history and source of the statute, short summaries (often referred to as **annotations**) of federal and state court opinions and Florida attorney general opinions interpreting the statute, and citations to relevant secondary sources and West key numbers. The hardbound volumes of *Florida Statutes Annotated* are updated by **pocket parts**. Pocket parts are used to update a fair number of law books in the law library. The pocket part is generally located inside the back cover of a hardbound volume. A pocket part contains any new material not contained in the hardbound volume. From time to time the hardbound volume is reprinted, incorporating material both from the hardbound volume and the pocket part.

The text of the Florida constitution is found in the last volume of *Florida Statutes* as well as volumes toward the end of *Florida Statutes Annotated.* Annotated court rules are found in volumes toward the end of *Florida Statutes Annotated.* West Group annually publishes a paperbound volume **Florida Rules of Court—State** containing the current Florida court rules and the Florida Evidence Code. The Florida Evidence Code comprises chapter 90 of the *Florida Statutes* and can also be found in *Florida Statutes* and *Florida Statutes Annotated.*

Proposed Florida administrative regulations, notices of public hearings on proposed regulations, notices of emergency rulemaking actions, and notices of filings are found in **Florida Administrative Weekly**. *Florida Administrative Weekly* is published once a week in newsletter form. Regulations are codified in the **Florida Administrative Code,** a loose-leaf publication. The *Florida Administrative Code* is updated by replacing loose-leaf pages containing outdated material with updated pages. **Florida Administrative Law Reports**, published since January 1979, is the official reporter of many Florida administrative agencies. It contains orders of administrative agencies and appellate court decisions concerning Florida administrative agencies.

Secondary sources

Secondary sources you might use to research Florida law include **Florida Jurisprudence 2d**, **American Law Reports** annotations, legal periodicals, law review articles, and continuing education publications.

Figure 3

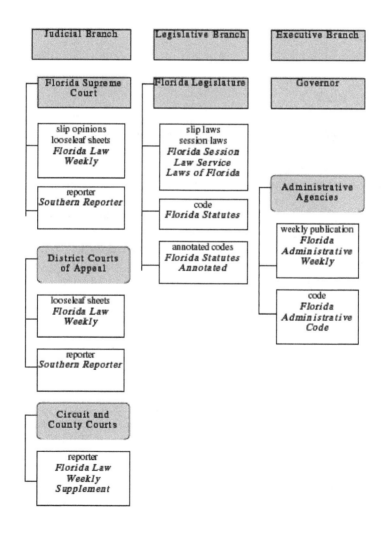

Florida Jurisprudence 2d is the state's legal encyclopedia. Much like material in any other encyclopedia, material in *Florida Jurisprudence 2d* is organized alphabetically by topic. *Florida Jurisprudence 2d* is updated by pocket parts.

The Florida Bar publishes the **Florida Bar Journal**, a legal periodical containing articles on Florida law. The Florida Bar also publishes many continuing education publications. Each Florida law school publishes a law review or law journal. Law reviews and law journals are legal periodicals edited by second- and third-year law students.

Finding tools

Finding tools used in researching Florida law include **Florida Digest 2d, Shepard's Florida Citations, Shepard's Southern Citations**, and the **Index to Legal Periodicals**. *Florida Jurisprudence 2d* and *American Law Reports* are often used as finding tools to find primary sources and other secondary sources.

Florida Digest 2d uses the West Group **key number system** and functions as an index to Florida cases. The digest contains more than 400 topics, each divided into subtopics identified by key numbers. Each subtopic in the digest is followed by single paragraph notes, with each note summarizing a legal principle from a case. A relevant case can be found by reading the notes under an applicable topic and using the case citation at the end of the paragraph to locate the case.

Shepard's Florida Citations and *Shepard's Southern Citations* contain lists of other cases, and of legal publications citing a published Florida case or a Florida statute. Florida law libraries usually contain either *Shepard's Southern Citations* or *Shepard's Florida Citations*. *Shepard's Southern Citations* contains information on cases and statutes from Alabama, Florida, Louisiana, and Mississippi, while *Shepard's Florida Citations* contains information only on Florida cases and statutes. *Shepard's Citations* should be consulted

∞   to determine whether a case or statute is still good law;
∞   whether a case has been affirmed, reversed, or overruled; or
∞   whether a statute has been amended, repealed, or declared unconstitutional.

Computer-assisted legal research

If available, legal research may also be performed using the computer. Computer-assisted legal research includes the use of online services. Some of the online services such as **Westlaw®**, **LexisNexis®**, and **VersusLaw®** are fee-based databases that require a password for access. Other services accessible through the Internet, such as FindLaw, are free.

Appendix B contains a list of websites helpful to someone who would like to perform legal research online. Appendix E contains questions concerning a number of the websites.

Legal research exercises

Appendixes C and D contain legal research questions regarding Florida cases and Florida statutes, some of which your professor may ask you to complete. The questions may be answered either in your institution's law library or online, using the websites listed in Appendix B. When a question asks for the authority for your answer, you should give the correct citation to the source of your answer. Rule 9.800 of the Florida Rules of Appellate Procedure contains sample citations to a wide range of sources. You can formulate correct citations by referring to Rule 9.800.

Fla. R. App. P. 9.800.

Rule 9.800. UNIFORM CITATION SYSTEM

This rule applies to all legal documents, including court opinions. Except for citations to case reporters, all citation forms should be spelled out in full if used as an integral part of a sentence either in the text or in footnotes. Abbreviated forms as shown in this rule should be used if the citation is intended to stand alone either in the text or in footnotes.

    (a) Florida Supreme Court

        1) 1846-1886: *Livingston v. L'Engle*, 22 Fla. 427 (1886).
        2) *Fenelon v. State*, 594 So. 2d 292 (Fla. 1992).
        3) For recent opinions not yet published in Southern Reporter, cite to Florida Law Weekly: *Traylor v. State*, 17 Fla. L. Weekly S42 (Fla. Jan. 16, 1992). If not therein, cite to the slip opinion; *Medina v. State*, No. SC00-280
           (Fla. Mar. 14, 2002).

    (b) Florida District Courts of Appeal.

        1) *Sotolongo v. State*, 530 So. 2d 514 (Fla. 2d DCA 1988); *Buncayo v. Dribin*, 533 So. 2d 935 (Fla. 3d DCA 1988).
        2) For recent opinions not yet published in Southern Reporter, cite to Florida Law Weekly: *Myers v. State*, 16 Fla. L. Weekly D1507 (Fla. 4th DCA June 5, 1991). If

not therein, cite to the slip opinion: *Fleming v. State*, No. 1D01-2734 (Fla. 1st DCA Mar. 6, 2002).

(c) Florida Circuit Courts and County Courts.

    1) *Whidden v. Francis*, 27 Fla. Supp. 80 (Fla. 11th Cir. Ct. 1966).

    2) *State v. Alvarez*, 42 Fla. Supp. 83 (Fla. Dade Cy. Ct. 1975).

    3) For opinions not published in Florida Supplement, cite to Florida Law Weekly: *State v. Campeau*, 16 Fla. L. Weekly C65 (Fla. 9th Cir. Ct. Nov. 7, 1990). If not therein, cite to the slip opinion: *State v. Campeau*, No. 90-4363 (Fla. 9th Cir. Ct. Nov. 7, 1990).

(d) Florida Administrative Agencies. (Cite if not in Southern Reporter.)

    1) For decisions of the Public Employees Relations Commission: *Indian River Educ. Ass'n v. School Board*, 4 F.P.E.R. ¶ 4262 (1978).

    2) For decisions of the Florida Public Service Commission: *In re Application of Tampa Elec. Co.*, 81 F.P.S.C. 2:120 (1981).

    3) For decisions of all other agencies: *Insurance Co. v. Department of Ins.*, 2 F.A.L.R. 648-A (Fla. Dept. of Insurance 1980).

(e) Florida Constitution. (Year of adoption should be given if necessary to avoid confusion.) Art. V, § 3(b)(3), Fla. Const.

(f) Florida Statutes (Official). § 350.34, Fla. Stat. (1973). § 120.53, Fla. Stat. (Supp. 1974).

(g) Florida Statutes Annotated. (To be used only for court-adopted rules, or references to other nonstatutory materials that do not appear in an official publication.) 32 Fla. Stat. Ann. 116 (Supp. 1975).

(h) Florida Laws. (Cite if not in Fla. Stat. or if desired for clarity or adoption reference.)

1) After 1956: Ch. 74-177, § 5, at 473, Laws of Fla.
2) Before 1957: Ch. 22000, Laws of Fla. (1943).

(i) Florida Rules.
Fla. R. Civ. P. 1.180.
Fla. R. Jud. Admin. 2.035.
Fla. R. Crim. P. 3.850.
Fla. R. Work. Comp. P. 4.113.
Fla. Prob. R. 5.120
Fla. R. Traf. Ct. 6.165.
Fla. Sm. Cl. R. 7.070.
Fla. R. Juv. P. 8.070.
Fla. R. App. P. 9.100.
Fla. R. Med. 10.010.
Fla. R. Arb. 11.010.
Fla. Fam. L. R. P. 12.010.
Fla. Admin. Code R. 62D-2.014.
R. Regulating Fla. Bar 4-1.10.
Fla. Bar Found. By-Laws, art. 2.19(b).
Fla. Bar Found. Charter, art. III, § 3.4.
Fla. Bar Integr. R., art. XI, § 11.09.
Fla. Jud. Qual. Comm'n R. 9.
Fla. Std. Jury Instr. (Civ.) 6.4(c).
Fla. Std. Jury Instr. (Crim.) 2.03.
Fla. Std. Jury Instr. (Crim.) Robbery
Fla. Stds. Imposing Law. Sancs. 9.32(a).
Fla. Bar Admiss. R. 3-23.1.

(j) Florida Attorney General Opinions. Op. Att'y Gen. Fla. 73-178 (1973).

(k) United States Supreme Court. *Sansone v. United States*, 380 U.S. 343 (1965). (Cite to United States Reports, if published therein; otherwise cite to Supreme Court Reporter, Lawyer's Edition, or United States Law Week, in that order of preference. For opinions not published in these reporters or in the United States Law Week, cite to Florida Law Weekly Federal: *California v. Hodari D.*, 13 Fla. L. Weekly Fed. S249 (U.S. Apr. 23, 1991).

(1) Federal Courts of Appeals. *Gulf Oil Corp. v. Bivins*, 276 F.2d 753 (5th Cir. 1960). For opinions not published in the

Federal Reporter, cite to Florida Law Weekly Federal: *Cunningham v. Zant*, 13 Fla. L. Weekly Fed. C591 (11th Cir. March 27, 1991).

(m) Federal District Courts. *Pugh v. Rainwater*, 332 F. Supp. 1107 (S.D. Fla. 1971). For opinions not published in the Federal Supplement, cite to Florida Law Weekly Federal: *Wasko v. Dugger*, 13 Fla. L. Weekly Fed. D183 (S.D. Fla. Apr. 2, 1991).

(n) United States Constitution. Art. IV, § 2, cl. 2, U.S. Const. Amend. V, U.S. Const.

(o) Other citations. When referring to specific material within a Florida court's opinion, pinpoint citation to the page of the Southern Reporter where that material occurs is optional, although preferred. All other citations shall be in the form prescribed by the latest edition of The Bluebook: A Uniform System of Citation, The Harvard Law Review Association, Gannett House, Cambridge, MA 02138. Citations not covered in this rule or in The Bluebook shall be in the form prescribed by the Florida Style Manual published by the Florida State University Law Review, Tallahassee, Fla. 32306.

(p) Case Names. Case names shall be underscored (or italicized), in text and in footnotes.

The Internet
∞   A basic tutorial on searching the Web:
     http://www.sc.edu/beaufort/library/pages/bones/bones.shtml

Starting Points (directory sites)

∞   Cornell Law School Legal Information Institute:
     http://www.law.cornell.edu/
∞   Washburn University School of Law's Washlaw Web:
     http://www.washlaw.edu/
∞   Findlaw: http://www.findlaw.com/
∞   LexisNexis (fee-based, password protected):
     http://www.lexisnexis.com
∞   Westlaw (fee-based, password protected):
     http://www.westlaw.com
∞   VersusLaw (fee-based, password protected):
     http://versuslaw.com
∞   Florida Law Online: http://www.floridalawonline.net

Information

∞   About Florida state courts: http://www.flcourts.org
∞   About the Florida Supreme Court:
     http://www.floridasupremecourt.org
∞   About the Florida Legislature: http://www.leg.state.fl.us
∞   About the Florida Senate: http://www.flsenate.gov
∞   About the Florida House: http://www.myfloridahouse.gov/
∞   About the Florida Bar: http://www.floridabar.org/
∞   About federal courts: http://www.uscourts.gov/
∞   About Congress: http://thomas.loc.gov/
∞   About the United States Senate: http://www.senate.gov
∞   About the United States House of Representatives:
     http://www.house.gov/

∞   About the United States Supreme Court:
http://www.supremecourtus.gov

∞   About the White House: http://www.whitehouse.gov

Florida law (sites containing primary sources)

∞   Florida Supreme Court opinions:
http://www.floridasupremecourt.org

∞   Opinion from other Florida state courts:
http://www.flcourts.org

∞   Florida Law Weekly: http://www.floridalawweekly.com/

∞   Florida constitution and Florida statutes:
http://www.flsenate.gov

∞   Florida administrative law:
http://election.dos.state.fl.us/fac/index.shtml

∞   Attorney general opinions: http://www.myfloridalegal.com/

Federal law (sites containing primary sources)

∞   United States Supreme Court opinions—Cornell Law School
Legal Information Institute: http://www.law.cornell.edu/

∞   Opinions from lower federal courts—Emory Law Library
Federal Courts Finder: http://www.law.emory.edu/FEDCTS/

∞   Federal statutes: http://www4.law.cornell.edu/uscode/

Legal Research Search Engines

∞   LawCrawler: http://lawcrawler.findlaw.com (Findlaw search
tool)

∞   Meta-index for U.S. legal research:
http://gsulaw.gsu.edu/metaindex/

∞   Lawguru: http://www.lawguru.com/search/lawsearch.html

∞   All Law—Your Internet Legal Gateway:
http://www.AllLaw.com/

Case law questions: Answer the following questions using *Southern Reporter* and Rule 9.800 of the Florida Rules of Appellate Procedure.

1. In 2006, the Florida Supreme Court decided whether Judge Sloop should be disciplined.
    a. What is the proper citation to this case?
    b. What were the activities that were the basis of the charges against Judge Sloop?
    c. What was the result in the case?

2. In 2006, the Florida Supreme Court decided whether Judge Downey should be disciplined.
    a. What is the proper citation to this case?
    b. What were the activities that were the basis of the charges against Judge Downey?
    c. What was the result in the case?

3. In 2006, the Florida Supreme Court decided whether Judge Renke should be disciplined.
    a. What is the proper citation to this case?
    b. What were the activities that were the basis of the charges against Judge Renke?
    c. What was the result in the case?

4. In 2006, the Florida Supreme Court decided whether Judge Adams should be disciplined.
    a. What is the proper citation to this case?
    b. What were the activities that were the basis of the charges against Judge Adams?
    c. What was the result in the case?
    d. Why didn't the Florida Supreme Court impose a more severe discipline?

5. In 2005, the Florida Supreme Court decided whether Judge Henson should be disciplined.

    a.   What is the proper citation to this case?

    b.   What were the activities that were the basis of the charges against Judge Henson?

    c.   What was the result in the case?

6. In 2005, the Florida Supreme Court decided whether Judge Diaz should be disciplined.

    a.   What is the proper citation to this case?

    b.   What were the activities that were the basis of the charges against Judge Diaz?

    c.   What was the result in the case?

7. In 2005, the Florida Supreme Court decided whether Judge Allawas should be disciplined.

    a.   What is the proper citation to this case?

    b.   What were the activities that were the basis of the charges against Judge Allawas?

    c.   What was the result in the case?

    d.   What was the basis for the discipline recommended by the Judicial Qualifications Commission?

8. In 2004, the Florida Supreme Court decided whether Judge Angel should be disciplined.

    a.   What is the proper citation to this case?

    b.   What were the activities that were the basis of the charges against Judge Angel?

    c.   What was the result in the case?

9. In 2001, the Florida Supreme Court decided whether Judge McMillan should be disciplined.

    a.   What is the proper citation to this case?

    b.   What were the activities that were the basis of the charges against Judge McMillan?

    c.   What was the result in the case?

10. In 2002, the Florida Supreme Court decided whether Judge Baker should be disciplined.
    a. What is the proper citation to this case?
    b. What was the activity that was the basis of the charge against Judge Baker?
    c. What was the result in the case?

11. In 2000, the Florida Supreme Court decided whether Judge Shea should be disciplined.
    a. What is the proper citation to this case?
    b. What were the activities that were the basis of the charges against Judge Shea?
    c. What was the result in the case?

12. In 2003, the Florida Supreme Court decided whether Judge Cope should be disciplined.
    a. What is the proper citation to this case?
    b. What were the activities that were the basis of the charges against Judge Cope?
    c. What was the result in the case?

13. In 2003, the Florida Supreme Court decided whether Judge Schapiro should be disciplined.
    a. What is the proper citation to this case?
    b. What were the activities that were the basis of the charges against Judge Schapiro?
    c. What was the result in the case?

14. In 1962, the Florida Supreme Court attempted to define what conduct constituted the practice of law in *State ex rel. Florida Bar v. Sperry.*
    a. What is the proper citation to this case?
    b. How did the Florida Supreme Court define conduct constituting the practice of law?

15. In 2004, the Florida Supreme Court determined whether We
The People Forms And Service Center of Sarasota, Inc. had
been engaged in the unauthorized practice of law.
   a. What is the proper citation to this case?
   b. What acts did We The People Forms And Service
      Center of Sarasota, Inc. engage in that allegedly
      constituted the unauthorized practice of law?
   c. What did the Florida Supreme Court decide, and why?

16. In 2002, the Florida Supreme Court determined whether
Neiman had been engaged in the unauthorized practice of
law.
   a. What is the proper citation to this case?
   b. What acts did Neiman engage in that allegedly
      constituted the unauthorized practice of law?
   c. What did the Florida Supreme Court decide, and why?

17. In 2002, the Florida Supreme Court determined whether
Abreu had been engaged in the unauthorized practice of law
when he dealt with immigration matters.
   a. What is the proper citation to this case?
   b. What acts did Abreu engage in that allegedly
      constituted the unauthorized practice of law?
   c. What did the Florida Supreme Court decide, and why?

18. In 2002, the Florida Supreme Court determined whether
Hughes had been engaged in the unauthorized practice of
law.
   a. What is the proper citation to this case?
   b. What findings did the court make regarding what
      Hughes had done?
   c. What punishment was imposed?

19. In 1999, the Florida Supreme Court determined whether
Eubanks and others had been engaged in the unauthorized
practice of law.
   a. What is the proper citation to this case?
   b. What acts did Eubanks and others engage in that
      allegedly constituted the unauthorized practice of law?
   c. What was the result?

20. In 2006, the Florida Supreme Court determined whether
    D'Ambrosio had violated attorney ethics rules.
    a. What is the proper citation to this case?
    b. What rules was D'Ambrosio charged with violating?
    c. What were the actions that allegedly violated the
       rules?
    d. What punishment was imposed?

21. In 2006, the Florida Supreme Court determined whether
    Tobkin had violated attorney ethics rules.
    a. What is the proper citation to this case?
    b. What rules was Tobkin charged with violating?
    c. What were the actions that allegedly violated the
       rules?
    d. What punishment was imposed?

22. In 2006, the Florida Supreme Court determined whether
    Feige had violated attorney ethics rules.
    a. What is the proper citation to this case?
    b. What rules was Feige charged with violating?
    c. What were the actions that allegedly violated the
       rules?
    d. What punishment was imposed?

23. In 2005, the Florida Supreme Court determined whether
    Gross had violated attorney ethics rules.
    a. What is the proper citation to this case?
    b. What rules was Gross charged with violating?
    c. What were the actions that allegedly violated the
       rules?
    d. What punishment was imposed?

24. In 2005, the Florida Supreme Court determined whether
    Stein had violated attorney ethics rules.
    a. What is the proper citation to this case?
    b. What rules was Stein charged with violating?
    c. What were the actions that allegedly violated the
       rules?
    d. What punishment was imposed?

25. In 2005, the Florida Supreme Court determined whether Forrester had violated attorney ethics rules.
    a. What is the proper citation to this case?
    b. What rules was Forrester charged with violating?
    c. What were the actions that allegedly violated the rules?
    d. What punishment was imposed?

26. In 1996, the Florida Supreme Court determined whether Wasserman had violated attorney ethics rules.
    a. What is the proper citation to this case?
    b. What were the actions that allegedly violated the rules?
    c. What punishment was imposed?

27. In 2002, the Florida Supreme Court determined whether Van Zamft had violated attorney ethics rules.
    a. What is the proper citation to this case?
    b. What rule was Van Zamft charged with violating?
    c. What was the action that allegedly violated the rule?
    d. What punishment was imposed?

28. In 2002, the Florida Supreme Court determined whether Massari had violated attorney ethics rules.
    a. What is the proper citation to this case?
    b. What were the actions that allegedly violated the rule?
    c. What punishment was imposed?

29. In 2001, the Florida Supreme Court determined whether John A. Barley had violated attorney ethics rules.
    a. What is the proper citation to this case?
    b. What were the actions that allegedly violated the rule?
    c. What punishment was imposed?

30. In 2004, the Florida Supreme Court decided *B.C. v. Florida Department of Children and Families.*
    a. What is the proper citation to this case?
    b. What was the certified issue before the court?
    c. What did the Florida Supreme Court hold?
    d. What did the court look to in determining legislative intent?

31. In 2004, the Florida Supreme Court decided *R.J. Reynolds Tobacco Co. v. Kenyon.*
    a. What is the proper citation to this case?
    b. What did the district court refuse to do?
    c. What did the Florida Supreme Court hold?
    d. Does Rule 9.330(a) require the district court to issue an opinion?

32. In 2005, the Florida Supreme Court decided *Tippens. v. State.*
    a. What is the proper citation to this case?
    b. What does Art. V, § 3(b)(3) of the Florida constitution require to afford the Florida Supreme Court jurisdiction?
    c. What did the Florida Supreme Court hold in *Tippens*?
    d. Why did the court lack jurisdiction in each of the three consolidated cases?

33. In 2006, the Florida Supreme Court decided *Jackson v. State.*
    a. What is the proper citation to this case?
    b. What was the issue before the court?
    c. What did the Florida Supreme Court hold?
    d. What was the court's reasoning?
    e. What did the court direct the clerk's office to do in similar cases?

34. In 1998, the Florida Supreme Court decided *Chiles v. Phelps.*
    a. What is the proper citation to this case?
    b. What did the Florida Supreme Court decide was one of its primary judicial functions?
    c. What did the Florida Supreme Court hold?

35. In 1994, the Florida First District Court of Appeal decided *In re Court Divisions.*
    a. What is the proper citation to this case?
    b. What were the two divisions of the court?
    c. How would the divisions operate with respect to each other?

36. In 1994, the Florida Supreme Court determined whether the circuit courts or the county courts had equity jurisdiction in *Alexdex Corp. v. Nachon Enterprises, Inc.*
    a. What is the proper citation to this case?
    b. What did the Florida Supreme Court decide?

37. In 2002, the Florida Fourth District Court of Appeal decided *Florida Dept. of Agriculture and Consumer Services v. Haire,* a case concerning Rule 9.125.
    a. What is the proper citation to this case?
    b. What was the issue in the case?
    c. What was the subject matter of the case?
    d. What did the court decide, and why?

38. In 2002, the Florida Supreme Court decided *White v. Steak and Ale of Florida, Inc.*
    a. What is the proper citation to this case?
    b. How did the court gain jurisdiction of the case?
    c. What was the issue in the case?
    d. What did the Florida Supreme Court decide?

39. In 1991, the Florida Supreme Court decided *State v. Tillman.*
    a. What is the proper citation to this case?
    b. What was the subject matter of the case?
    c. What did the Florida Supreme Court decide, and why?

40. In 2002, the Florida Supreme Court decided *Caulfield v. Cantele.*
    a. What is the proper citation to this case?
    b. When may a Florida District Court of Appeal hear an appeal?
    c. What was the issue in the case?

41. In 1998, the Florida Fifth District Court of Appeal decided
    Burns v. Hacker.

    a. What is the proper citation to this case?

    b. What was the issue?

    c. What did the court decide, and why?

42. In 1996, the Florida Fourth District Court of Appeal decided
    Leahy v. Batmasian.

    a. What is the proper citation to this case?

    b. Did the Florida Fourth District Court of Appeal have
        jurisdiction over the case? Why or why not?

43. In 2002, the Florida Supreme Court stated a rule in *Ferguson
    v. State* that determined whether a court ruling was retroactive
    in effect.

    a. What is the proper citation to this case?

    b. What was the rule?

44. In 2002, the Florida Supreme Court determined in *State v.
    Klayman* whether a prior case was retroactive in application.

    a. What is the proper citation to this case?

    b. What was the holding of the prior case?

    c. Was the prior case retroactive in application? Why or
        why not?

    d. What was the result for Klayman?

45. In 2002, the Florida Supreme Court determined in *Bunkley v. State* whether a prior case was retroactive in application. In 2003, the United States Supreme Court vacated the judgment in *Bunkley.*
    a. What is the proper citation to this case in the Florida Supreme Court?
    b. What was the holding in the prior case?
    c. According to the Florida Supreme Court, was the prior case retroactive in application? Why or why not?
    d. What is the proper citation to this case in the United States Supreme Court?
    e. Why did the United States Supreme Court disagree?
    f. What was the result for Bunkley?

46. In 1994, the Florida Supreme Court decided *Department of Revenue v. Kuhnlein.*
    a. What is the proper citation to this case?
    b. What were the plaintiffs claiming?
    c. What is the standing requirement under Florida law?
    d. Did the plaintiffs have standing?

Questions on statutes: Answer the following questions using Florida Statutes and Rule 9.800 of the Florida Rules of Appellate Procedure.

1.
   a. Is it legal for a minor to purchase a lottery ticket in Florida?
   b. What is the authority for your answer?

2.
   a. When is it illegal to sell a lottery ticket in Florida?
   b. What is the authority for your answer?

3.
   a. How many terms does the Florida Supreme Court have annually, and when do the terms begin?
   b. What is the authority for your answer?

4.
   a. May a retired Florida Supreme Court justice practice law?
   b. What is the authority for your answer?

5.
   a. How are jurors summoned to serve in Florida state court?
   b. What happens if one requests that jury service be postponed?
   c. What is the penalty for failing to serve as a juror when summoned?
   d. What is the authority for your answer?

6.
   a. What is the length of service of a trial juror (petit juror)?
   b. What is the authority for your answer?

7.

    a. What is the statute of limitations for filing a lawsuit based on a contract?

    b. What is the authority for your answer?

8.

    a. What is the statute of limitations for filing a lawsuit based on negligence?

    b. What is the authority for your answer?

9.

    a. What is the statute of limitations for filing a lawsuit based on legal malpractice?

    b. What is the authority for your answer?

10.

    a. What is the residence requirement to obtain a divorce (dissolution of marriage) in Florida?

    b. What is the authority for your answer?

11.

    a. In Florida, who may be adopted, and who may adopt?

    b. What is the authority for your answer?

12.

    a. What is the fine for driving thirty miles per hour over the speed limit?

    b. What is the authority for your answer?

13.

    a. What is the duty of someone involved in an automobile accident resulting in someone's death?

    b. What is the penalty for not fulfilling this duty?

    c. What is the authority for your answer?

14.
   a. What is the minimum blood-alcohol level to be considered
      driving under the influence?
   b. What is the authority for your answer?

15.
   a. What is the maximum size container in which beer can be sold
      in Florida?
   b. What is the authority for your answer?

16.
   a. What is the reduction in the fee for obtaining a marriage
      license if the couple completes a premarital preparation
      course?
   b. What is the authority for your answer?

17.
   a. Is it legal for an employer in Florida to pay someone a lower
      wage because of the person's sex, race, or age?
   b. What is the authority for your answer?

18.
   a. Does Florida recognize the tort of breach of a contract to
      marry?
   b. What is the authority for your answer?

19.
   a. What is the liability of a dog owner?
   b. What is the authority for your answer?

20.
   a. Can a Good Samaritan be liable for civil damages to someone
      injured?
   b. What is the authority for your answer?

21.
   a. Why would a newspaper publish a retraction of and apology
      for incorrect information previously published?
   b. What is the authority for your answer?

22.

    a. What is a vehicular homicide?

    b. What is the authority for your answer?

23.

    a. What is an assault?

    b. What is the authority for your answer?

24.

    a. Is it a crime to repeatedly contact someone via email?

    b. What is the authority for your answer?

25.

    a. Is it illegal for an unmarried couple to live together?

    b. What is the authority for your answer?

26.

    a. Is it illegal for an unmarried person to marry someone already married?

    b. What is the authority for your answer?

27.

    a. Is it illegal for someone to send a note to someone, threatening to kill or injure the person?

    b. What is the authority for your answer?

28.

    a. Can someone be guilty of perjury simply for making two contradictory statements?

    b. What is the authority for your answer?

29.

    a. What is the defense to perjury?

    b. What is the authority for your answer?

30.

    a. May a minor obtain a tattoo?

    b. What is the authority for your answer?

APPENDIX E

Website Questions

Use the Florida Supreme Court website at
http://www.floridasupremecourt.org to answer the following
questions:

1. Who are the Justices of the Florida Supreme Court?

2. List three pieces of information available through the public
    information section of the website.

3. What are three questions frequently asked of the Florida Supreme
    Court and what are the answers to those questions?

4. What are three questions frequently asked of the Florida Supreme
    Court clerk's office and what are the answers to those questions?

5. List three pieces of information available through the oral
    argument section of the website.

6. When does the clerk's office typically release opinions of the
    Florida Supreme Court?

Use the Florida State Courts website at http://www.flcourts.org to
answer the following questions:

1. How many judges usually sit to hear a case in a Florida District
    Court of Appeal?

2. What is the name of the Florida state trial-level court that hears
    misdemeanor cases?

3. What is the name of the Florida state trial-level court that hears misdemeanor cases?

4. What is the name of the Florida state trial-level court that hears felony cases?

5. Name the Florida District Court of Appeal serving your area and give the URL of the court's website.

6. Name the city that serves as the headquarters for the District Court of Appeal.

7. Describe three types of useful information that one can obtain from the District Court of Appeal website.

8. Name the Florida Circuit Court serving your area and give the URL of the court's website.

9. Name the chief circuit judge of the circuit.

10. Name three services provided by the circuit.

Use the Florida Legislature website at http://www.leg.state.fl.us to find the answers to the following questions:

1. Name the president of the Florida Senate and the speaker of the Florida House of Representatives.

2. Name your Florida state senator and Florida state representative. (If you are unsure where the district lines fall, guess in which district you live.)

3. What is the deadline for the governor of Florida to sign a bill?

4. How can you tell the difference between a House bill and a Senate bill?

Use the Federal Courts website http://www.uscourts.gov/ to answer the following questions:

1. Name the number of the regional circuit of the United States Court of Appeals covering Florida, and give the URL of the court's website.

2. Describe a newsworthy piece of information found at the court's website.

3. Name the United States District Court serving your area and give the URL of the court's website.

4. Describe a newsworthy piece of information found at the court's website.

5. Who appoints federal judges?

6. What is the filing fee for filing a civil case in the United States District Court?

The website for Congress is http://thomas.loc.gov/. Use it to answer these questions:

1. What is meant by the numeric designation of a Congress (for example the 110th Congress), and what is a session of Congress?

2. What information can be obtained by searching "Bill Summary & Status"?

3. What is the salary of United States senators and representatives?

The website for the United States Senate is http://www.senate.gov. Use it to answer these questions:

1. Name the senators from Florida.

2. When will the Senate next convene?

3. From the Senate organization chart, what is the name of the president pro tempore?

4. From the Senate organization chart, what is the name of the floor majority leader?

5. From the Senate organization chart, what is the name of the floor minority leader?

6. From the Senate organization chart, what is the name of the floor majority whip?

7. From the Senate organization chart, what is the name of the floor minority whip?

The website for the United States House of Representatives is http://www.house.gov/. Use it to answer these questions:

1. Name your representative in the United States House of Representatives.

2. What is the name of the speaker of the House?

3. What is the name of the floor majority leader?

4. What is the name of the floor minority leader?

5. What is the name of the floor majority whip?

6. What is the name of the floor minority whip?

Use the United States Supreme Court website at http://www.supremecourtus.gov to answer the following questions:

1. Name the present members of the United States Supreme Court.

2. What is the name of the most recent slip opinion decided by the United States Supreme Court?

3. What are the qualifications for being admitted to practice before the United States Supreme Court?

4. Read through the Visitor's Guide to Oral Argument at the Supreme Court of the United States. What are four noteworthy pieces of information found in the guide?

ENDNOTES

[1] Betsy L. Stupski, Florida Legal Research 1-3, 1-9, 1-10 (5th ed. 1998).

[2] Art. III, § 1, Fla. Const.

[3] Art. III, § 3, Fla. Const.

[4] Art. IV, § 1, Fla. Const.

[5] Art. IV, § 5, Fla. Const.

[6] Stupski, *supra* note 1, at 1-3.

[7] Supreme Court of Florida 23 (December 1994). This book was obtained from the Office of the State Courts Administrator. It was printed by the State of Florida "for the purpose of informing the general public about the operations and facilities of the Supreme Court of Florida and the Florida judicial system." *Id.* inside back cover.

[8] Art. V, § 1, Fla. Const.

[9] Stupski, *supra* note 1, at 1-3; Art. XI, §§ 2, 5, Fla. Const.

[10] Art. XI, § 2, Fla. Const.

[11] Art. II, § 3, Fla. Const.; § 20.02, Fla. Stat. (2006).

[12] §§ 20.02, 20.201, 20.43, Fla. Stat. (2006).

[13] 28 U.S.C.S. §§ 1331, 1332 (2003).

[14] Art. V, § 3 (b)(6), Fla. Const.

[15] 28 U.S.C.S. § 89 (2001); FLA. B.J. 541 (Sept. 1999).

[16] 28 U.S.C.S. §§ 41, 43, 48 (2001).

[17] 28 U.S.C.S. §§ 1254, 1257 (2001).

[18] Resolution of the Florida State-Federal Judicial Council Regarding Calendar Conflicts between State and Federal Courts (Jan. 13, 1995).

[19] Fla. R. Jud. Admin. 2.450.

[20] Art. V, § 17, Fla. Const.; § 27.015, Fla. Stat. (2006).

[21] § 27.02, Fla. Stat. (2006).

[22] § 27.03, Fla. Stat. (2006).

[23] § 27.05, Fla. Stat. (2006).

[24] § 27.181, Fla. Stat. (2006).

[25] Art. V, § 17, Fla. Const.

[26] Art. V, § 18, Fla. Const.; § 27.50, Fla. Stat. (2006).

[27] §§ 27.51, 27.53, Fla. Stat. (2006).
[28] § 27.5303, Fla. Stat. (2006).
[29] §§ 27.51(5)(a), 27.702, Fla. Stat. (2006).
[30] Art. V, § 2(a), Fla. Const.
[31] Fla. R. Civ. P. 1.010. For civil traffic infractions in Traffic Court, *also see* Florida Rules of Traffic Court.
[32] Fla. Prob. R. 5.010.
[33] Fla. Sm. Cl. R. 7.010, 7.020.
[34] Fla. R. Traf. Ct. 6.160; Fla. R. Crim. P. 3.010.
[35] Fla. Fam. L. R. P. 12.005.
[36] Fla. Fam. L. R. P. 12.010.
[37] Fla. Fam. L. R. P. 12.020.
[38] Fla. Fam. L. R. P. 12.010(2).
[39] Fla. Fam. L. R. P. Fm. 12.900(a)-12.994(b).
[40] Fla. Evid. C. §§ 90.401 - 90.403, 90.801 - 90.903 (2006).
[41] Fla. Evid. C. §§ 90.501 - 90.507 (2006).
[42] *In re Amendments to the Florida Evidence Code*, 914 So. 2d 940 (Fla. 2005).
[43] Fla. R. App. P. 9.010.
[44] Fla. R. App. P. 9.030, 9.210, 9.320, 9.370.
[45] Fla. R. Jud. Admin. 2.140(b).
[46] Fla. R. Jud. Admin. 2.120, 2.215 (e).
[47] Art. I, § 15 (a), Fla. Const. (emphasis added).
[48] §§ 905.01, 905.16, 905.23, 905.24, Fla. Stat. (2006).
[49] Art. I, § 22, Fla. Const.
[50] §§ 69.071, 73.071 (1), Fla. Stat. (2006).
[51] § 913.10, Fla. Stat. (2006).
[52] Fla. R. Crim. P. 3.440.
[53] §§ 40.01, 40.011, Fla. Stat. (2006).
[54] § 40.013, Fla. Stat. (2006).
[55] Fla. R. Civ. P. 1.431; Fla. R. Crim. P. 3.300 - 3.350.
[56] Fla. R. Jud. Admin. 2.320.
[57] *In re McMillan*, 797 So. 2d 560, 562 (Fla. 2001).
[58] *In re Baker*, 813 So. 2d 36, 37-38 (Fla. 2002).
[59] Art. V, § 15, Fla. Const.; § 454.021, Fla. Stat. (2006).
[60] § 454.11, Fla. Stat. (2006).
[61] Ch. 455, Fla. Stat. (2006).
[62] R. Regulating Fla. Bar 1-2.
[63] Fla. R. Jud. Admin. 2.510.

[64] R. Regulating Fla. Bar 3-5.1.

[65] Gary Blankenship, *Grievance group gears up for year-long examination*, FLA. B. NEWS, Oct. 1, 2003, at 1.

[66] Florida Bar disciplinary statistics are accessible from the Florida Bar's website at http://www.floridabar.org.

[67] R. Regulating Fla. Bar 5-1.1.

[68] Fla. Bar Found. Charter, art. III, § 2.1(h).

[69] Florida Bd. of Bar Examiners ex rel. Chavez, 894 So.2d 1 (Fla. 2004).

[70] *Lawyer gets 10 years for misusing client funds*, FLA. B. NEWS, Mar. 1, 2002, at 14.

[71] R. Regulating Fla. Bar 6-3.5.

[72] Section 7 of the Uniform Administrative Policies and Procedures of the Civil Division of the Circuit Court Orange County, Florida, revised November 2006 [hereinafter the *Orange County Local Rules*].

[73] The website of Paralegal Association of Florida, Inc. is located at http://pafinc.org. The website of the National Association of Legal Assistants is located at http://nala.org/.

[74] Mark D. Killian, *Transitional panel created in anticipation of paralegal rule*, FLA. B. NEWS, Oct. 15, 2006, at 16.

[75] R. Regulating Fla. Bar 10-2.1.

[76] § 454.23, Fla. Stat. (2004).

[77] Gary Blankenship, *Citizens assist the Bar's UPL efforts*, FLA. B. NEWS, Dec. 15, 2006, at 19.

[78] R. Regulating Fla. Bar, 7-1.1.

[79] Gerard Shields, *Bar investigates unlicensed law practitioners: Critics say lawyers too expensive for many*, ORLANDO SENTINEL, August 2, 1995, at C-3.

[80] Gary Blankenship, *UPL investment, overhaul net results for consumers*, FLA. B. NEWS, Nov. 1, 1999, at 6; *A UPL Snapshot*, FLA. B. NEWS, Dec. 15, 2006, at 19.

[81] Gary Blankenship, *Lawmakers invite tougher UPL sanctions*, FLA. B. NEWS, Oct. 15, 2003, at 1.

[82] *UPL Actions*, FLA. B. NEWS, July 1, 2005, at 27.

[83] R. Regulating Fla. Bar 10-7.2.

[84] Loretta C. O'Keefe, *Engaging in UPL can land you behind bars*, FLA. B. NEWS, June 15, 2004, at 22.

[85] *Police raid home: Bar asks court to hold UPL suspects in contempt,* FLA. B. NEWS, September 15, 1994, at 7.

[86] *UPL nets Toca two years,* FLA. B. NEWS, Sept. 1, 1998, at 1.

[87] *FDLE makes UPL arrest,* FLA. B. NEWS, April 1, 2004, at 6.

[88] *Man sentenced for UPL,* FLA. B. NEWS, April 15, 2005, at 12.

[89] Art. V, §§ 1, 7, Fla. Const.

[90] Fla. Sm. Cl. R. 7.010; Fla. R. Traf. Ct. 6.010.

[91] *White v. State,* 446 So. 2d 1031, 1035 (Fla. 1984); *Shaw v. Shaw,* 334 So. 2d 13, 16-17 (Fla. 1976).

[92] *Walter v. Walter,* 464 So. 2d 538, 539-40 (Fla. 1985).

[93] Art. V, §§ 3, 4, 5, Fla. Const.

[94] Art. V, §§ 3(b), 4(b), 5(b), Fla. Const.

[95] §§ 775.08, 775.081, 775.083, Fla. Stat. (2006).

[96] Art. I, § 16, Fla. Const.

[97] Fla. R. Crim. P. 3.191.

[98] Art. I, § 21, Fla. Const.

[99] §§ 318.13, 318.18, Fla. Stat. (2006).

[100] §§ 57.081, 57.085, Fla. Stat. (2006).

[101] §§ 47.011, 47.051, Fla. Stat. (2006).

[102] *Forms and Surfaces, Inc. v. Welbro Constructors, Inc.,* 627 So. 2d 594, 595 (5th DCA 1993).

[103] *Manrique v. Fabbri,* 493 So. 2d 437, 440 (Fla. 1986).

[104] § 47.061, Fla. Stat. (2006).

[105] § 47.011, Fla. Stat. (2006).

[106] § 47.091-47.122, Fla. Stat. (2006).

[107] Art. I, § 16, Fla. Const.

[108] Fla. R. Crim. P. 3.240.

[109] Art. V, § 6, Fla. Const.

[110] §§ 34.01, 34.011, Fla. Stat. (2006).

[111] § 34.022, Fla. Stat. (2006).

[112] Art. V, § 8, Fla. Const.; § 34.021, Fla. Stat. (2006).

[113] Art. V, § 13, Fla. Const.

[114] Art. V, § 10, Fla. Const.

[115] Art. V, § 11, Fla. Const.

[116] Fla. R. Jud. Admin. 2.220.

[117] Fla. Sm. Cl. R. 7.010.

[118] Fla. Sm. Cl. R. 7.020.

[119] Fla. Sm. Cl. R. 7.140.

[120] Fla. Sm. Cl. R. 7.050.
[121] Fla. Sm. Cl. R. 7.060.
[122] Fla. Sm. Cl. R. 7.090.
[123] Fla. R. Traf. Ct. 6.010.
[124] Fla. R. Traf. Ct. 6.160.
[125] § 318.32, Fla. Stat. (2006).
[126] § 318.14, Fla. Stat. (2006); Traf. Ct. R. 6.100.
[127] § 318.14, Fla. Stat. (2006).
[128] Art. V, § 1, Fla. Const.; Traf. Ct. R. 6.630.
[129] §§ 318.30 - 318.32, 318.34, Fla. Stat. (2006); Traf. Ct. R. 6.630.
[130] § 26.01, Fla. Stat. (2006).
[131] § 26.012, Fla. Stat. (2006); Art. V, § 5, Fla. Const.
[132] Fla. R. Civ. P. 1.100.
[133] Fla. R. Jud. Admin. 2.515.
[134] Fla. R. Jud. Admin. 2.520.
[135] § 26.031, Fla. Stat. (2006).
[136] Art. V, §§ 8, 10, Fla. Const.
[137] Art. V, § 10, Fla. Const.
[138] Art. V, § 8, Fla. Const.
[139] Art. V, § 13, Fla. Const.
[140] Art. V, § 11, Fla. Const.
[141] § 26.57, Fla. Stat. (2006).
[142] Art. V, § 2, Fla. Const.; Fla. R. Jud. Admin. 2.215.
[143] § 26.55, Fla. Stat. (2006).
[144] Section 3 of the Orange County Local Rules; § 26.20, Fla. Stat. (2006).
[145] Fla. R. Civ. P. 1.200, 1.490.
[146] Art. V, § 16, Fla. Const.
[147] § 26.49, Fla. Stat. (2006).
[148] §§ 28.211, 28.241, 28.29, Fla. Stat. (2006).
[149] § 30.15, Fla. Stat. (2006).
[150] R. Jud. Admin. 2.535.
[151] Section 2 of the Orange County Local Rules.
[152] *Family Court Initiative Moves Ahead, Ready for Future,* Full Court Press, July - August 1995, at 1 - 2.
[153] *Id.* at 8-15.
[154] *Id.* at 18.
[155] *Id.* at 9.
[156] *Id.* at 10.

[157] § 39.401, Fla. Stat. (2006).
[158] *Family Court Initiative Moves Ahead, Ready for Future*, Full Court Press, July - August 1995, at 11.
[159] *Id.* at 12.
[160] *Id.* at 13.
[161] *Id.* at 13 - 14 (emphasis added).
[162] Fla. Fam. L. R. P. 12.490, Form 12.920.
[163] Fla. R. Civ. P. 1.490.
[164] Fla. R. Juv. P. 8.255.
[165] § 35.01, Fla. Stat. (2006).
[166] § 35.05, Fla. Stat. (2006).
[167] Art. V, § 4(b), Fla. Const.
[168] Fla. R. App. P. 9.200.
[169] Fla. R. App. P. 9.210.
[170] Fla. R. App. P. 9.320.
[171] § 35.13, Fla. Stat. (1993); Art. V, § 4, Fla. Const.
[172] Fla. R. App. P. 9.331.
[173] § 35.06, Fla. Stat. (2006).
[174] Art. V, § 8, Fla. Const.
[175] Art. V, § 13, Fla. Const.
[176] Art. V, § 11, Fla. Const.
[177] Art. V, § 10, Fla. Const.
[178] Art. V, § 2, Fla. Const.
[179] Art. V, § 4 (c), Fla. Const.
[180] §§ 35.22 - 35.25, Fla. Stat. (2006); Fla. R. App. P. 9.040 (g), 9.100, 9.110.
[181] § 35.26, Fla. Stat. (2006).
[182] Art. II, § 2, Fla. Const.
[183] Art. V, § 3 (b), Fla. Const.
[184] Art. IV, § 1(c), Fla. Const.
[185] Art. IV, § 10, Fla. Const.
[186] Blankenship, *Grimes says courts must work to educate the public*, FLA. B. NEWS, July 15, 1995, at 20.
[187] Supreme Court Manual of Internal Operating Procedures, Introduction.
[188] Supreme Court Manual of Internal Operating Procedures, Sections III, IV, V.
[189] Art. V, §§ 3, 8, Fla. Const.
[190] Art. V, § 13, Fla. Const.

[191] Art. V, § 11, Fla. Const.

[192] Art. V, § 10, Fla. Const.

[193] Art. V, § 3(a), Fla. Const.

[194] Art. V, § 2, Fla. Const.

[195] Supreme Court Manual of Internal Operating Procedures, Section I.

[196] Fla. R. Jud. Admin. 2.225.

[197] Art. V, §§ 10, 11, Fla. Const.

[198] *See* the Supreme Court Judicial Nominating Commission Rules of Procedure, the Uniform Rules of Procedure for District Courts of Appeal Judicial Nominating Commissions, and the Uniform Rules of Procedure for Circuit Judicial Nominating Commissions.

[199] Art. V, § 12, Fla. Const.

[200] Fla. Jud. Qual. Comm'n R. 21.

[201] *In re Andrews*, 875 So.2d 441 (Fla. 2004).

[202] Jan Pudlow, *Court removes Judge Sloop*, FLA. B. NEWS, Jan. 1, 2007, at 19.

[203] Art. III, §17, Fla. Const.

[204] § 44.1011 (2), Fla. Stat. (2006).

[205] Fla. R. Arb. 11.030 (b).

[206] § 44.1011 (1), Fla. Stat. (2006).

[207] § 44.201 (3), Fla. Stat. (2006).

[208] Section 15 of the Orange County Local Rules.

[209] Fla. R. Civ. P. 1.700 - 1.730; Fla. Fam. L.R.P. 12.740 – 12.741.

[210] Fla. R. Med. 10.810, 10.830.

[211] §§ 44.103, 44.104, Fla. Stat. (2006); Fla. R. Civ. P. 1.700 (a).

[212] Fla. R. Arb. 11.010, 11.020.

[213] Fla. R. Civ. P. 1.820.

[214] Fla. R. Civ. P. 1.830; § 44.104, Fla. Stat. (2006).

[215] Fla. R. Civ. P. 1.830.

[216] § 44.201, Fla. Stat. (2006).

[217] http://orangecountybar.org.

original jurisdiction
  defined, 19–20

P

paralegals. *See* legal assistant
parent orientation courses
  defined, 33
peremptory challenge
  defined, 9
petit jury
  defined, 8
petition
  defined, 28
petition for writ of certiorari, 3
plaintiff
  defined, 21
pleadings
  affirmative defense, 28
  answer to complaint or petition, 28
  answer to counterclaim, 26
  answer to crossclaim, 28
  briefs, 34
  complaint, 28
  counterclaim, 28
  crossclaim, 28
  final judgments, 30
  interlocutory orders, 34
  notice of appeal, 36
  orders of dismissal, 30
  petition, 28
  reply, 28
  third-party answer, 28
  third-party complaint, 28
  transcript, 30
  verification, 28
pocket parts
  defined, 54
presentment
  defined, 8
pretrial conference
  defined, 26
primary sources
  defined, 50
privilege
  conversations
    defined, 6–7
  waiver

  defined, 7
pro se assistance services
  defined, 32
pro se litigants, 13
  defined, 32
probate
  defined as civil matter, 21
  jurisdiction of circuit court, 27
Probate Rules, 6
  defined, 6
procedural law
  defined, 5
public defenders
  defined, 4–5
public record
  defined, 8

Q

qualification for retention
  appellate judges, 36
  circuit judges, 29
  county court judge, 24
  Supreme Court justices, 42
question of law
  certifying, 2
questions of law
  determination by judge, 19

R

real property
  title and boundaries
    jurisdiction of circuit court, 27
removal to federal courts, 2
reply
  defined, 28
reporter of decisions
  defined, 42
reporters
  defined, 51
  Southern Reporter, 51, 53, 55
representation by attorney
  requirements, 13
reversible error
  defined, 19
Rule 4-1.1 Competence, 50

matters of great public
  importance, 37
validity of state statutes, 37
Supreme Court (Florida)
  adoption of court rules, 5
  adoption of Florida Evidence
    Code, 7
  approved legal forms, 14–15
  authorization under Florida
    Constitution, 19
  chief justice role at impeachment,
    45–46
  death penalty dominance in cases,
    38
  generally, 37–43
  governing by Rules of Appellate
    Procedure, 7
  jurisdiction, 37–38
    death penalty, 37
  justices
    generally, 42
    retention, 42
  opinions, 41–42, 55
  personnel, 42–43
    clerk of the Supreme Court, 42
    executive assistant, 42
    Librarian of the Supreme Court,
      42
    marshal of the Supreme Court,
      42
    staff attorneys, 42
    staff of the chief justice, 42
    State Courts Administrator, 42
  procedure, 38–42
  removal of judges, 44–48
  sitting in divisions, 19
  unauthorized practice of law, 16-
    18
Supreme Court Library
  defined, 42
Supreme Court Manual of Internal
  Operating Procedures, 38–42
  electronic recordings and
    broadcasts, 40
  opinions, 41–42
  oral argument procedures, 39–40
  pre-argument procedures, 38–39
  recusals, 40–41

release of opinions to public, 41–
  42
Supreme Court Nominating
  Commission
  defined, 43

T

tax assessment
  jurisdiction of circuit court, 27
teen court
  defined, 33
third-party complaint
  defined, 28
Toca, Jesse
  unauthorized practice of law, 18
tort
  defined, 21
traffic court
  defined, 6
  generally 26–27
  rules
    defined, 6
traffic courts
  as division of county court, 19
  defined, 26
traffic infractions
  civil
    defined, 26
    hearing officer
      defined, 26
  defined as civil matter, 21
traffic offenses
  criminal
    defined, 26
traffic violations bureau
  defined, 26
transcript
  defined, 30
trial
  bench, 19
  by jury, 19
trial by jury
  guarantee by Florida Constitution,
    8, 21
trial clerks
  defined, 31
trial courts